STARS IN A
DARK NIGHT

Ivor Gurney (1890–1937)

STARS IN A DARK NIGHT

The Letters of IVOR GURNEY
to the Chapman Family

ANTHONY BODEN

With a Foreword by
MICHAEL HURD

SUTTON PUBLISHING

This book was first published in 1986 by
Sutton Publishing Limited · Phoenix Mill
Thrupp · Stroud · Gloucestershire · GL5 2BU

This new revised edition first published in 2004 by
Sutton Publishing Limited.

British Library Cataloguing in Publication Data
A catalogue record for this book is available from the
British Library.

ISBN 0 7509 3467 0

Typeset in 12/14pt Photina.
Typesetting and origination by
Sutton Publishing Limited.
Printed and bound in Great Britain by
J.H. Haynes & Co. Ltd, Sparkford.

*In Memory
of
Donald Johnson*

CONTENTS

Kitty, Micky, Arthur and Winnie Chapman.
Drawing by Clara Simmons, 1912

FOREWORD

In one of his shortest but most moving poems, Ivor Gurney wrote prophetically: 'There are bright tracks/Where I have been.' Yet even he, I think, would have been astonished at how bright and glowing those tracks were to become. When he died, on 26 December 1937, the prospects seemed dim indeed. But friends who knew him and believed in him as a composer and poet, kept faith and in their turn inspired those who could only know him through his work – though to know an artist through his work is to know him as he would wish to be known. Now with nearly one hundred magnificent songs (many of them recorded), a splendidly authoritative collection of over three hundred poems, a volume of his War Letters, and a full-scale biography to hand, he suddenly appears in his true light as one of the most important figures of his generation – a creative genius of rare quality, and a singularly attractive human being.

Although the facts of Gurney's life are undeniably tragic, it should be remembered that he had a genius for friendship and a great capacity to enjoy his friends. That aspect of his life has remained somewhat in the shadows for lack of any great weight of documentary evidence. But Anthony Boden's newly discovered collection of his letters to the Chapman family restores the balance. They are not letters of worldly consequence, but, more importantly, the record of warmth and human kindness, quiet courage and dignity of spirit – written, for our delight, with a musician's ear and a poet's sensibility.

Michael Hurd
West Liss, Hampshire
1986

Author's Prefatory Note

In the eighteen years that have passed since the appearance of the first edition of *Stars in a Dark Night*, Ivor Gurney's personal star has continued to rise without interruption. The large numbers attending a Summer Weekend of English Music and Verse that I organised in Gloucester in 1990 to celebrate the centenary of Gurney's birth gave a clear indication of an increasing interest in his extraordinarily creative talent. Several further editions of Gurney's poetry have been published since then, as have a substantial collection of his letters and additional volumes of his music. Gurney's poems are now to be found in numerous anthologies, including *The Oxford Book of English Verse*. There is a flourishing Ivor Gurney Society and an Ivor Gurney website (www.Ivor.Gurney.net). He has found a permanent place in English degree courses; the number of theses and learned articles written about him and his work continues to grow rapidly; and P.J. Kavanagh's revised edition of the *Collected Poems* has recently been published.[1] Gurney has come into his own, his reputation secure.

Anthony Boden
2004

1 P.J. Kavanagh (ed.), *Ivor Gurney: Collected Poems* (Fyfield Books/ Carcanet, 2004).

A Note on the Text

All the letters and documents in this collection were found amongst the possessions of Winifred Miles (Winnie) and of her sister Marjorie Freeman (Micky). Winnie died in 1982 and Micky in 1979; their sister Kitty in 1963, and their brother Arthur in 1954 whilst playing cricket.

Only very rarely did Gurney date his letters. However, for this revised edition I have, in the main, followed the date order adopted by Kelsey Thornton, who has transcribed most of this correspondence into his *Ivor Gurney: Collected Letters* (MidNAG Carcanet, 1991). At the head of the letters I have indicated how the date has been arrived at with a letter:

G indicates that Gurney gives a date.
P indicates that the postmark tells the date (though it is possible that one or two letters may have been returned to wrong envelopes).
KT indicates Kelsey Thornton's conclusion about the date.
AB indicates my own conclusion about the date.

ACKNOWLEDGEMENTS

I would like to express my gratitude to Michael Hurd and P.J. Kavanagh for their pioneering work on Gurney and for their valuable advice, both when this book was first in preparation and since. I am indebted to Kelsey Thornton, David Johnson, Christian Wilson and the late Mrs Joy Finzi for their help and encouragement; the Trustees of the Imperial War Museum, London, for the right to publish the six photographs taken in France during the First World War; Mrs Gwynneth Hargeaves for the photograph of Chosen Hill, Gloucestershire; Mr and Mrs I.M. Fraser, the residents of St Michael's, High Wycombe in 1985, for permission to photograph their home; Ivan Sparkes, the Librarian at High Wycombe for the photograph of Christ Church in the town; Chatto & Windus Ltd for permission to quote from the late Leonard Clark's bibliographical note to *The Poems of Ivor Gurney 1890–1937*; and, not least, I am extremely grateful to Chris Gorringe for rescuing my computer when it crashed at a late stage in my work on this book.

I was also indebted to the late J.R. Haines, one of my predecessors as Trustee of the Ivor Gurney Estate, who generously consented to give me open access to the Gurney Archive in the Gloucester City Library, and to the Oxford University Press for permission to quote the poems from P.J. Kavanagh's *Collected Poems of Ivor Gurney*.

I am grateful to Sarah Flight, my editor at Sutton Publishing, for giving me the opportunity to revise this book, and to my wife, Anne, for her constant support and encouragement.

Above all, I treasure the memory of my mother-in-law, the late Winifred Miles (*née* Chapman), whose affectionate recollections of Ivor Gurney moved me to write of his friendship with her family.

The Songs I Had

The songs I had are withered
Or vanished clean,
Yet there are bright tracks
Where I have been.

And there grow flowers
For others' delight.
Think well, O singer,
Soon comes night.

INTRODUCTION

'Lend me your back, Winnie!'

Such was the request made by Ivor Gurney of his young companion as they walked through the woodland at Burnham Beeches in Buckinghamshire one day in 1919. Winnie stopped and offered her back as a writing-surface, just as she had done many times before on those long country walks with Ivor that she enjoyed so much. Taking a small music manuscript book from his pocket, he began silently to write down what he had been composing in his head. Winnie felt the gentle pressure on her back; and felt too a pride in the companionship of this young man. She was nineteen years old, and he twenty-eight. As he finished writing, he whispered quietly, 'One day I shall be famous, Winnie'.

This small incident was never forgotten by Winifred Miles (*née* Chapman), whose affection for Ivor Gurney remained unfaded to the end of her life in 1982. But Gurney was not to enjoy fame in his lifetime. His biographer, Michael Hurd[1] has described the upbringing and life of the man who was blessed with

---

[1] Michael Hurd, *The Ordeal of Ivor Gurney* (OUP, 1978; paperback 1984).

rare gifts as both poet and composer, especially of songs, but whose joyous spirit, for the last fifteen years of his life, was abandoned to the torment of an asylum.

Ivor Bertie Gurney was born at 3 Queen Street, Gloucester, on 28th August 1890, the second child of four: an elder sister, Winifred Marion; a brother, Ronald Edward; and the youngest, Dorothy Evelyn. His father, David Gurney, although a tailor by trade, was a countryman at heart, born in the Severnside village of Maisemore, close to Gloucester. Ivor's mother, Florence (*née* Lugg), was a highly strung, domineering woman who helped in the family business at 3 Queen Street, a property which was both shop and home.

The old cathedral city was to remain at the heart of Gurney's inspiration; the focus of his natural creative genius. Much of Gurney's Gloucester has been swept away, victim to the onrush of ill-advised post-World War Two development that was to homogenise so many ancient English cities. Queen Street is no more, replaced by a featureless covered walkway at the side of Boots the chemist, where a small plaque marks Gurney's birthplace. Nonetheless, the ancient Roman shape of Gloucester remains, and in the cathedral close it is still possible to see and to sense a place where 'Gloucester history seems/A living thing and an intense'.[2]

Whilst Ivor was still a babe in arms David and Florence Gurney took a small step up the social ladder, moving the family home out of Queen Street and into larger shop premises at 19 Barton Street. This property has also been replaced, and the section of Barton Street

---

[2] Ivor Gurney, 'The Old City – Gloucester'.

in which it stood absorbed into the city's Eastgate. Winifred Gurney recorded her memories of growing up above the tailor's shop:

Ours was a business home – not bright and cheerful – the rooms being [of] secondary consideration to the shop premises and workshop. So there was 'nowhere to lay one's head', so to speak. Bell ringing from the shop, little space to allow for study or quiet reflection and relaxation for any of us, to say nothing about Ivor [. . .]

Our parents were old fashioned, reserved and undemonstrative, not conducive to drawing out the warmest affections. My father was by far the most home loving, affectionate parent and was our favourite. Stern when necessary, but kindly. He hated to punish any of us, but we knew where we stood at once. My mother cared thoroughly for our material needs, but lost sight of the fact [that] if no seeds of love were planted, no fruit could be forthcoming. So our regards for Father were strong, and he enjoyed being with us, but Ivor was very kindly disposed to his mother in spite of all drawbacks.

Ivor loved his father and loved to be with him, especially when he took us out into the country very often. Both my parents were country bred and born, and loved the country. They both appreciated beauty: my father more noticing the birds, wild flowers, *etc.*, and Mother would go into raptures over a beautiful sunset. Both were musical. Mother had a little musical education but Father had not. They both loved [the] good music of the cathedral, and we were brought up in that atmosphere.

My parents were God-fearing people of the old school. It was cold lunch on Sundays and church most of the time. Father hated us to be invited out for anything on Sundays and rarely allowed us to go. Later, not being a reader, I upset him very much by either cleaning my bicycle or sewing machine on a Sunday, which I felt a great urge to do rather than sit and be miserable.

Father was very fond of romping with us [. . .] He often took us on his knees and shook us till our teeth rattled or chattered, and the worst thing I endured was what we knew as 'a rough shave'. He rubbed our faces with his rough chin. Still, we loved all this, and, like Oliver Twist, asked for more until play became painful [. . .] He was, I suppose, not perfect but he could cook better than Mother, and he always rose first in the morning and lit the fire, chopped the wood and such things. It was not often that Mother could afford domestic help, though at times it was necessary. She was not always fit, being also neurotic, but lived till she was 85. She was definitely Spartan, and took the comfort and love out of life. [3]

Elsewhere, she was to write that:

Happiness revolved around father. As very small children mother certainly did her best to bring us up well, but when we grew to be more independent it seemed too much for her. She possessed us as babies, but couldn't do so later and her iron rule led to

[3] Gurney Archive, Gloucester City Library (hereafter referred to as 'GA'), 78.24. Letter from Winifred Gurney to Don Ray.

nagging. Life for us was something akin to a bed of stinging nettles, and to keep the peace father's efforts had to be applied when and where possible, but taking care to walk warily [. . .] The pity of it was that mother did not seem to enjoy her children, and so far as I could see she did not win their love. Worse still, Father was not allowed to give us as much love as he had for us [. . .]. [4]

David and Florence Gurney had met at their local church, All Saints, Barton Street, where they both sang in the choir and where David's cousin Joseph was the organist. When they brought Ivor to All Saints for baptism on 24 September 1890, neglecting to invite any of their friends or relations to sponsor the child, the vicar, the Reverend Herbert Foster, agreed to stand as one of Ivor's godparents; his young curate, the Reverend Alfred Hunter Cheesman, the other. This proved to be a stroke of singular good fortune. Cheesman, a bachelor and philanthropist who helped many Gloucester boys from poor backgrounds to establish themselves in life, took his godfatherly responsibilities towards Ivor extremely seriously.

As a youngster, Gurney attended the National School in Gloucester's London Road, and when he was eight, joined the choir at All Saints. It soon became obvious that he had musical ability, and in 1900, urged on by Cheesman, he successfully secured a place in the Gloucester Cathedral choir – and with it, full-time education at the King's School. As young Gurney grew,

---

[4] Michael Hurd, *op cit*, p. 11. Winifred Gurney reminiscences.

The Reverend Alfred Hunter Cheesman at The Rectory, Twigworth,
Gloucestershire

Cheesman gathered him under his wing, gave the boy open access to his considerable library; lent him books; introduced him to fine poetry, prose and history; and encouraged him in his education and music.

It may well have been Cheesman who introduced Gurney to the Misses Emily and Margaret Hunt, who lived at 54 Wellington Street, a short walk from the Gurney shop. Both were professional musicians; Emily was a pianist and Margaret a violinist, and they had taught music in South Africa in the years before the Boer War. On settling in Gloucester they had continued to teach piano and violin, and for Gurney, their home, like Cheesman's, was a place not just of learning, but of inspiration and sanctuary, so utterly different from 19 Barton Street. There, whenever she heard Ivor playing pieces that were not strictly prescribed for his piano practice, his mother would stand at the bottom of the stairs and shout up that she knew very well that the music was not part of his lesson. In the tranquillity of the Hunts' home his creative spirit was nurtured and encouraged. By 1904 he was already composing, and within three years had determined that his life was to be spent in the service of music.

Unsurprisingly, Gurney began to spend more and more of his time in homes other than his own. Between 1905 and 1911 he visited Cheesman almost every day.[5] According to Winifred, 'he practically lived with him'. Ivor's visits to the Hunt sisters were frequent, and, in addition to the pleasures of music making and conversation with them, he was to discover the beauties of the Cotswolds in their company.

[5] GA 61.86. Letter, 19 April 1937: Alfred Cheesman to Marion Scott.

Gurney had a great capacity for friendship; his boyhood circle was expanding – but throughout his life he only ever found time for people of a like sensitivity to his own. Winifred Gurney remembered that, 'Ivor had several boy friends to whom he dedicated music [. . .] they would have to be quite a genuine type or he would instantly drop them. Nothing sneakish or underhand would pass Ivor'.[6] One such boy who remained a lifelong friend, Frederick Saxty, lived near the Hunts in Wellington Street, and, in spite of his generally solitary nature, Ivor made many friends at the King's School. Although only an average pupil, he loved cricket, football and hockey, and enjoyed the musical life of the school and the cathedral. But, given his artistic temperament, there were bound to be boys who thought him an oddity. It has been said that some of his fellow pupils laughed at him and called him 'Batty Gurney',[6] a taunt almost invited by Ivor's second name, Bertie, pronounced 'Bartie'; indeed, his nickname in later life was 'Bartholomew'.[7]

[. . .] Ivor always seemed in a dream. More often than not he would be walking down the gutter as if looking for something, his cap all sideways, peak over one eye [. . .]

He had his occasions when I think he did not always agree with his playmates, but at one time it was a rule for several of the Cathedral Choir boys to come to tea on Sundays and walk four miles to

---

[6] Michael Hurd, *op cit*, p. 17.
[7] David Gurney had served his apprenticeship in Wimborne Minster, Dorset, where the local lord of the manor was Sir Ivor Bertie Guest.

Ivor Gurney, *c.* 1906

Maisemore with us to take Grandmother her weekly butter and tea. We went by road, by River Severn and sometimes through the woods, especially at bluebell time in spring. If they went out on weekdays, they played football and cricket, Father enjoying it quite as much as the boys.[8]

In 1906, Gurney became an articled pupil of Dr (later Sir) Herbert Brewer, the organist at the cathedral, remaining with him until 1911. Winifred Gurney remembered that Brewer 'found Ivor difficult at times':

Dr Brewer gave him little or no encouragement, according to what I had heard my father say. He did not appear to praise or do anything to help him, but told my father that he would be proud if the music that Ivor had written was his. I believe also that he took no part in Ivor's success at gaining the scholarship whatsoever, either by encouraging him go in for it or help[ing] him in his composition. This I think would definitely spur Ivor on to his goal without help and make him difficult with Dr Brewer.[9]

But there were consolations. In these years he forged two of his most important associations: with the poet F.W. Harvey (1888–1957), and with Herbert Howells (1892–1983), a fellow articled pupil with Brewer.[10]

---

[8] GA 78.25.
[9] GA 78.24.
[10] See Paul Spicer, *Herbert Howells* (Seren, 1998), and Anthony Boden, *F.W. Harvey: Soldier, Poet* (Sutton Publishing, 1988; 2/1998).

Gurney's close bond with Harvey began one day in 1908 when, on boarding a tram in Gloucester, he sat beside a young man whose face was vaguely familiar. A few words quickly established that both had attended the King's School, although in different classes. The conversation turned to music and poetry; to their love of football and cricket; to a shared passion for the English countryside, and particularly for Gloucestershire – and so began a lifelong friendship that was to be hugely influential on Gurney the future poet.

Will Harvey was reluctantly articled to a Gloucester solicitor. Whenever he could get away from his office, and Ivor could slip away from the cathedral, the two friends would go off together, sharing their discoveries and talking endlessly of music and books. A favourite place was Chosen Hill at Churchdown, close enough to the city to be reached easily, but far enough away to be blissfully tranquil. From the top of the little hill the view stretches away across the Severn Vale to the Malverns, the Cotswolds and Bredon; there are traces of an encampment from which the Romans kept watch over Gloucester, and a little church, St Bartholomew's, marks a place of worship older than Christianity. Will and Ivor felt themselves to be possessed by Gloucestershire.

Harvey's farmhouse home at Minsterworth, 'The Redlands', became a regular calling place for Gurney. Whenever possible, Ivor would delight in visiting Harvey and his family to help in the fields, to walk in the Severn meadows, to pick fruit in the orchard, to play 'ping-pong' on the long dining-room table or cricket with Will's brothers and friends, to set off with guns to bag rabbits for the pot, to make music, and always to talk.

F.W. (Will) Harvey, *c.* 1906

Through professional contacts in Gloucester Harvey met the solicitor John (Jack) Haines, himself a published poet and friend of poets. Gurney and Harvey were regular callers at Haines's office in King Street, and one can imagine that very little of the conversation was concerned with legal matters. Haines was a fine hockey player, eventually chairman of the Gloucester City Club and a member of the England Hockey Selection Committee. Will Harvey played regularly for the Gloucester City Thursday XI, and therefore his contacts with Haines – business, literary and sporting – were frequent. In addition, he was often invited to visit Haines's family home, 'Midhurst', in Green Lane, Hucclecote, just outside Gloucester, and doubtless Gurney often accompanied him there.

Haines was related to Catherine Abercrombie, the wife of the poet Lascelles Abercrombie, who in 1911 had moved into The Gallows at Ryton, a village to the south-east of Dymock in Gloucestershire. Abercrombie was the founder of a poets' colony that rented cottages in and around Dymock in 1914: the so-called 'Dymock Poets'. Included in their numbers were Rupert Brooke, John Drinkwater, Robert Frost, Wilfrid Gibson and Edward Thomas, and their presence in Dymock attracted other prominent literary figures, including W.H. Davies, Eleanor Farjeon, Arthur Ransome, and Edward Marsh, patron of the arts and publisher of the highly influential *Georgian Poetry* series, the first volume of which appeared in 1912.

The potential of such contacts, through Haines, must have seemed heaven-sent. Harvey was soon writing to Abercrombie, seeking advice on how to succeed as a poet; Gurney's contact was to be delayed by war.

Harvey and Gurney bought a little boat during a summer holiday that Ivor spent in the lock-keeper's cottage at Framilode, and the pair delighted in sailing her, sometimes recklessly, on the River Severn.

> The *Dorothy* was very small: a boat
> Scarce any bigger than the sort one rows
> With oars! We got her for a five-pound note
> At second-hand. Yet when the river flows
> Strong to the sea, and the wind lightly blows,
> Then see her dancing on the tide, and you'll
> Swear she's the prettiest little craft that goes
> Up-stream from Framilode to Bollopool.[11]

Herbert Howells came from Lydney, a small town in the Forest of Dean, the son of a tradesman whose business had failed. But Herbert's musical talent had been noticed; he was fortunate enough to attract the patronage of the local Squire, Charles Bathurst (First Viscount Bledisloe of Lydney, one-time Governor-General of New Zealand), whose generosity, from 1905, funded Howells's private piano lessons with Herbert Brewer. In 1909 Brewer accepted Howells as an articled pupil alongside Gurney – and perhaps surprisingly, a third young man, Ivor Davies, who was to go on to find fame and fortune as Ivor Novello.

Howells and Gurney were very contrasting characters: Howells short, good-looking, carefully dressed and precise in manner; Gurney bespectacled, often untidy, disorganised and fun-loving. Even so, they had much in common: an ambition to achieve

---

[11] From F.W. Harvey, 'The Ballad of River Sailing'. Boden, *op cit*, p. 22.

something worthwhile in music and to find fame, an appreciation of poetry and, not least, a deep love for Gloucestershire.

Strangely, Gurney often kept his especial friends in separate compartments, and it was not until 1919 that he introduced Harvey to Howells, even though his pursuits with both were very similar. Howells would later write that he had 'walked miles of Gloucestershire ways, with Gurney singing aloud phrases that would go into "the next song"'.[12] The two went to Churchdown often, climbing Chosen Hill to sit enraptured by the Gloucestershire landscape; 'Gurney used to point to the outlines of the hills and tell his friend that if he were not thereby inspired to try to immortalise that sight in music, something was wrong in the scheme of things'.[13] Churchdown was, in any case, close to Howells's heart: the home of his sweetheart and future wife, Dorothy Dawe, was there.

Howells's innate good sense and practicality enabled him to build a solid career and, despite ill-health, climb steadily to a respected position in the musical establishment. Gurney, for all his charm, possessed no such instinct. He remained his own blundering self, and to all intents and purposes opted out of the race. The impression [Gurney and Howells] made on Dr Brewer is significant. In 1931 when, three years after his death, his autobiography was published, it was found that he mentioned Howells with pride. He

[12] *Music & Letters*, Vol. XIX, No I (January 1938).
[13] Christopher Palmer, *Herbert Howells: A Centenary Celebration* (Thames, 1992), p. 49.

mentioned even the ubiquitous Ivor Novello. But he did not mention Gurney.[14]

If Brewer was unhelpful, Gurney could always count on Cheesman's unfailing support. Ivor hoped to read for a degree at Durham University, for which he needed to take the matriculation examination. Cheesman not only undertook to coach Ivor for this, but also accompanied him to Durham in September 1907 when he was required to sit the examination. *En route*, they visited the cathedrals of York, Lincoln, Norwich, Ely and Cambridge, as well as of Durham itself, where Cheesman arranged for Ivor to play the organ. The trip was both a marvellous adventure and a great success: Gurney passed the examination.

The year 1910 brought the Three Choirs Festival to Gloucester and with it a revelatory experience for Gurney and Howells. The Festival, which rotates annually between Hereford, Gloucester and Worcester, traces its origins to the early eighteenth century and holds a central place in English musical life.[15] *The Dream of Gerontius*, conducted by Elgar, was to be a highlight of the 1910 Festival. Howells asked Brewer if there were to be any new works performed that year. 'Yes', was the reply, 'a queer, mad work by an odd fellow from Chelsea'.[16] The 'odd fellow' in question was Ralph Vaughan Williams; the work, his

---

[14] Michael Hurd, *op cit*, p. 25.

[15] See Anthony Boden, *Three Choirs: A History of the Festival* (Sutton, 1992).

[16] Michael Hurd, *op cit*, p. 24. Herbert Howell's reminiscences.

Fantasia on a theme by Thomas Tallis, programmed to be performed immediately before *Gerontius*.

Both Gurney and Howells were present at the concert and were enormously excited by the *Tallis Fantasia*. In it, Vaughan Williams had successfully cast a bridge back to the Golden Age of English music, the age of the Tudors, and expressed himself in modern musical language that owed nothing to continental influences. The effect on both aspiring composers was overwhelming. After the concert they paced the streets of Gloucester together for the rest of the night, unable to sleep – a novel experience for Howells but not for his companion – from his early teens Gurney was prone to nocturnal rambling about the countryside, describing himself as a 'nightwalker'.

All three young men – Gurney, Howells and Harvey – became immersed in and influenced by the music and literature of the sixteenth and seventeenth centuries. Howells was to say that all through his life he had felt that he belonged to the Tudor period, and Harvey once exclaimed: ' I would love to be able to wear the colours of the Tudors – but here I am, dressed all in brown!'[17]

In 1911, in spite of Brewer's disapproval but with the encouragement of Cheesman, Ivor sat for an open scholarship to the Royal College of Music. Again he was successful and, subsidised by Cheesman, set off for London, presenting himself at the College for interview by Sir Hubert Parry, Sir Charles Stanford, Dr Walford Davies and Dr Charles Wood. The portfolio of music that he had submitted contained a number of his best songs, and Parry and Stanford had apparently

---

[17] Reminiscences of Eileen Griffiths (*née* Harvey).

Gloucester Three Choirs Festival, 1907. Festival breakfast at the New Inn. Ivor Gurney is standing, third from right on the back row. Edward

Elgar is sitting, fourth from left on second row with Herbert Brewer seated to his right.

discussed certain Schubertian characteristics and even a similarity of handwriting in them; wearing his small-lensed spectacles he also looked a little like the great Viennese composer. It is said that when Gurney entered the room one of the distinguished interviewers – probably Stanford – exclaimed, 'By God! It is Schubert!'

In the autumn term of 1911, Gurney enrolled as a student at the RCM, and soon after met Miss Marion Scott (1877–1953), a musician, music historian, editor of the RCM magazine, and Secretary of the RCM Union; she was immediately impressed:

> For one thing the boy was wearing a thick, dark blue Severn pilot's coat, more suggestive of an out-of-door life than the composition lesson with Sir Charles Stanford for which (by the manuscript tucked under his arm) he was clearly bound. But what struck me more was the look of latent force in him, the fine head with its profusion of light brown hair (not too well brushed!) and the eyes, behind their spectacles, were of the mixed colouring – in Gurney's case hazel, grey, green and agate – which Erasmus once said was regarded by the English as denoting genius. 'This,' I said to myself, 'must be the new composition scholar from Gloucester whom they call Schubert.[18]

Marion Scott, thirteen years Gurney's senior, was to become a tireless advocate on his behalf: a staunch friend and constant correspondent who gathered together all of his music and poems, who strove to

[18] *Music & Letters*, Vol. XIX, No. I, (January 1938).

bring many of them to publication, and who provided order in his otherwise largely disorganised life. It may also have been Marion Scott who helped Gurney to obtain the organ post at Christ Church, High Wycombe, which he held both before and after the Great War; an appointment that gave him an escape every weekend from his dingy lodgings in Fulham, and through which he met the Chapman family, to whom the letters in this book are addressed.

Edward Chapman had worked his way up the rank ladder of the Great Western Railway until, in 1913, he was appointed Chief Clerk to the Goods Manager at Paddington Station. He moved his family from Ealing to High Wycombe, where they took up residence in a solid Victorian semi-detached house called St Michael's in Castle Hill (the house was re-named 'Strawberry Patch' in recent years, and Castle Hill has become 'The Greenway'). He was a sensitive and highly intelligent man with a determination to do his very best for his family, to which end he worked extremely hard. He was churchwarden of Christ Church and, on meeting the shy new organist, was quick to offer Gurney the hospitality of his home each weekend, and later, even tried to secure a position with the GWR for him.

Mrs Matilda Chapman seems to have been the epitome of an Edwardian lady. She was respected by her neighbours and deeply loved by her family; set great store by her position in society and went to some expense to maintain it; held Christian virtue highly and was an excellent cook; and when she quarrelled with her husband it was usually about money. Her weakness appears to have been a tendency to hypochondria, and she also worried deeply about Gurney's fits of

Edward Chapman – 'Le Comte'

Matilda Chapman – 'La Comtesse'

Christ Church, High Wycombe, now demolished

depression and mood swings. Gurney found her a stately lady and gave her the affectionate nickname 'La Comtesse', in consequence of which, Mr Chapman became 'Le Comte'.

Ivor's delight was to play with the four Chapman children: Catherine (Kitty), Winifred (Winnie), Arthur and Marjorie. Because she was born in the same week that Mr and Mrs Chapman had been to see *The Mikado*, Marjorie was called little 'Mikadoo' as a baby, and later, 'Micky'. When Ivor Gurney entered their lives in 1914, the children's ages ranged from Kitty, the eldest at seventeen, to Micky, a mischievous seven-year-old; and although four very different personalities, they all shared an immediate affinity with their new weekend companion.

In 1913 Gurney suffered one of the frequent bouts of depression that were to dog him throughout life. Taking leave of absence from the RCM for a short while, he returned to Gloucestershire, finding restorative peace and energy once again in the lock-keeper's cottage at Framilode. It is therefore easy to understand his need for a more easily accessible escape from the pressures of the RCM and his cheerless Fulham lodgings; at St Michael's he found a perfect retreat.

Ivor brought to the Chapman children a wonderful mixture of fun and enlightenment that they were never to forget. There were games of cricket and ping-pong, long country walks and robust races. His talk was full of the wonder of music and literature. Winnie and Micky especially remembered him playing Bach preludes, Beethoven sonatas, and reading aloud from Masefield's *The Everlasting Mercy* to a young and enthralled audience. They also remembered the joy that Ivor shared with them whenever threads of inspiration were drawn together and, for the very first time, he would play a completed composition on the little French piano in their drawing room. One of their favourites amongst these works was his setting of W.B. Yeats's poem 'Down by the Salley Gardens'.

But not all of the talk and music at St Michael's was serious. Gurney's wonderful sense of humour brought delighted laughter from parents and children alike. The whole family, often with friends too, would gather round the piano and sing hilarious choruses to Ivor's accompaniment. A great favourite was the song 'Miss Bailey's Ghost', from the Cecil Sharp book of *English Folksongs*, during which Ivor would roll his eyes wildly

Kitty (third from right) with cousins and friends

and shiver with exaggerated fear whilst singing the 'O-ooh, Miss Bailey!' lines.

After supper, Ivor would often enjoy sitting by the open fire, wearing an old pair of Edward Chapman's slippers, smoking a churchwarden pipe, and talking. He would tell the gathered company about his beloved Gloucestershire: of Maisemore, Framilode, Minsterworth, Crickley, Cranham and Chosen Hill. There would be speculation about the outcome of the war, which cast its cloud over the future of Europe, and he would express his long-held belief in the United States of America as the hope for the return of stability to the world.

Herbert Howells had followed Gurney to the RCM in 1912. Both studied composition with Stanford; Howells becoming a firm favourite with the brilliant but irascible pedagogue whose students included Vaughan Williams, Gustav Holst, Arthur Bliss, John Ireland and many more. In later years, Stanford would say that of all his pupils Gurney was potentially 'the biggest man of them all – but the least teachable'.[19] Holst knew very well what being 'teachable' involved. Week after week he was to hear his distinguished teacher say: 'It won't do, me boy. It won't do.'

> This verdict acted like a tonic. He appreciated the way that Stanford insisted on sincerity, and he readily accepted the creed that a composer, however gifted, must learn his technique so completely that he can afford to forget it.[20]

[19] *Ibid.*
[20] Imogen Holst, *Gustav Holst: A Biography* (OUP, 1938; paperback, 1988), p. 11.

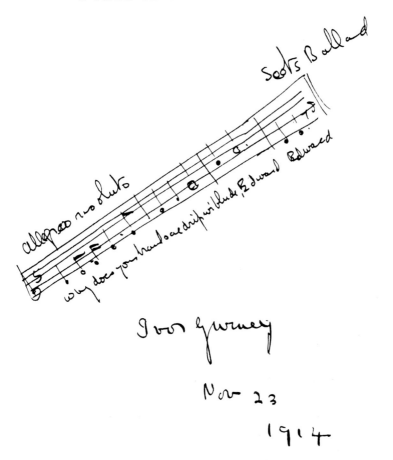

From Winnie's autograph book

Gurney's mind was less open to Stanford's creed: resistant to academic discipline and rigour, he was to have a hard time of it. Howells recalled vividly an occasion when Ivor had written a song of which he was particularly proud and took it along to a lesson with Stanford. Howells sat on the right side of the great man; Gurney on the left. Stanford gazed at the

From Winnie's autograph book

manuscript for a seemingly endless quarter of an hour, then took his gold propelling pencil from his waistcoat pocket and altered something. 'There, m'bhoy', he said, 'There, that'll be half-a-crown'. Gurney, infuriated, looked him straight in the eye and said, 'I see you've jiggered the whole thing!' Taking hold of Gurney by the scruff of his neck, Stanford shoved him out of the door, then leaned against the door, broke into a smile, and said, 'I love the boy more each time'![21]

Nonetheless, by 1914 Gurney had found both the Chapmans and his musical voice. He wrote excitedly to Will Harvey, who in the previous year had fallen in love with Sarah Anne Kane, a pretty Irish nurse who was to become his wife:

Dear Willy,

It's going Willy. It's going. Gradually the cloud passes and Beauty is a present thing, not merely an abstraction poets feign to honour.

Willy, Willy, I have done 5 of the most delightful and beautiful songs you ever cast your beaming eyes upon. They are all Elizabethan — the words — and blister my kidneys, bisurate my magnesia if the music is not as English, as joyful, as tender as any lyric of all that noble host. Technique all right, and as to word setting — models. 'Orpheus', 'Tears'. 'Under the Greenwood Tree'. 'Sleep', and 'Spring'. How did such an undigested clod as I make them? That, Willy, I cannot say. But there they are — Five Songs for Mezzo Soprano — 2 flutes, 2 clarinets, a harp and 2 bassoons, by Ivor Gurney, A.R.C.O. Yes, Willy, I got through that exam, and meningite my cerebralis if I didn't get Second Prize! [. . .].[22]

But then came war. Harvey was amongst the first to volunteer to fight, enlisting in the 1st/5th Battalion of the Gloucestershire Regiment. Determined to serve his

---

[21] See Christopher Palmer, *op cit*, pp. 352/3.
[22] GA: G.61.242.

country, Gurney made an unsuccessful attempt to join the Army in August 1914, but was rejected because of poor eyesight. By February of the following year the Army were less fussy; he tried again, and this time his application was accepted. He returned to Gloucester and spent a few unsuccessful weeks in the Gloucestershire Yeomanry – according to his sister Winifred, he had 'a rough time' of it with them – before transferring to 'B' Company, the 2nd/5th Battalion of the Gloucestershire Regiment and training as a signaller.

There is no doubt that Ivor Gurney was a patriot; but love of country was not his only motive in wishing to serve. He knew very well the fragility of his mental health and saw in the Army his chance to gain strength; to overcome the mental instability against which he struggled constantly. It is now thought likely that Gurney was suffering from manic depression (also known as bi-polar affective disorder), a condition involving extreme swings of mood, highs and lows, in which up to one in five sufferers are sufficiently tormented to contemplate suicide. Other diagnoses, including schizophrenia, have been suggested, but it is impossible to determine an accurate diagnosis at this distance. In any event, no effective treatment was available during Gurney's lifetime. But in some strange way the comradeship, discipline of arms, and extreme physical exertion did indeed seem to provide a pause in an inevitable decline from eccentricity to insanity.

In the trenches Gurney's creative energy was, in the main, channelled into writing poetry and letters to his many friends, there being very little opportunity for musical composition. The horror and waste of war appalled him, and yet, experiencing the extremity of human folly, he cried out for Truth and Beauty in some of his finest verse. All of these poems were sent back to Marion Scott, who, in no doubt about their quality, helped to arrange them into a volume which she submitted to Sidgwick & Jackson, the firm that, amongst others, had published the poems of Rupert Brooke and, in 1916, F.W. Harvey's first collection of poetry, *A Gloucestershire Lad at Home and Abroad*. Her efforts were rewarded, and in 1917 Sidgwick & Jackson published Gurney's first collection of verse under the title *Severn and Somme*, which was well received by the press.

The few songs that Gurney *was* able to write in the trenches and whilst 'at rest' behind the line are all amongst his best and, probably because he doubted that he would ever return to his beloved Gloucestershire alive, are often valedictory in feeling. They include his setting of Masefield's 'By a Bierside'; Sir Walter Raleigh's farewell to life, 'Even Such is Time'; 'In Flanders', a setting of a trench poem by Will Harvey, part of which is quoted to the Chapmans in one of the letters in this collection; and 'Severn Meadows', one of the few poems of his own that Gurney set to music:

> Only the wanderer
>   Knows England's graces,
> Or can anew see clear
>   Familiar faces.
>
> And who loves joy as he
>   That dwells in shadows?
> Do not forget me quite,
>   O Severn meadows.

Ivor Gurney and Herbert Howells, 1916

Gurney the habitual 'nightwalker' was always able to find a sense of oneness with nature in his solitary nocturnal wanderings. The figure of a lone, rootless wanderer is a recurrent theme in German Romantic art, and it is perhaps not too fanciful to suppose that Gurney identified himself with the isolated outsider who inhabits Schubert's magnificent settings of poems by Wilhelm Müller in the *Winterreise* cycle; in *Der Wanderer*, to a text by Schmidt von Lübeck; in the setting of Johann Seidl's poem *Der Wanderer an den Mond*, 'I wander a stranger, from land to land [. . .] yet, alas, nowhere am I at home'; or in the several settings of Goethe's *Wanderers Nachtlied*. In any event, it is remarkable that 'Severn Meadows', this poignant and best known of Gurney's songs, was written in the heat of war at Caulincourt, possibly whilst he and his comrades sheltered from enemy fire in the only building left standing in the town: a domed mausoleum.

Throughout the war, quiet home-thoughts and friendship in letters from the Chapmans sustained Gurney. He revelled in all their domestic doings, having found with them, for perhaps the first time, 'the homelife which is so strong and sweet a stimulant to any sound art'. St Michael's was also the focus of an even deeper feeling. From the first, Ivor had found his feelings for Kitty developing into an emotion much deeper than affection, and before he left for army training, proposed marriage. Kitty, a strong-willed girl of eighteen, would have none of it. She was far from ready for love, and had shared her fears with Winnie. When Ivor approached Edward Chapman he was told, albeit kindly, that Kitty was much too young to consider engagement. The relationship ended without rancour, and in 1916 Kitty joined the Land Army. She was sent to Syde in Gloucestershire and then, in 1917, to the Royal Farms at Windsor where she met her future husband, a young subaltern, Frank Johnson, who was training nearby; they married in 1921.

If Gurney wrote any letters to Kitty they have not survived, but she would have been included in his collective address, 'Dear Chapmen', and in 1919 he gave her a copy of John Masefield's *Salt-Water Ballads*, simply inscribed: 'To Kitty, with best wishes for Christmas 1919, from I.B.G.'. By then, however, he had been in love for a second time – and for a second time had been rejected.

Each summer the Chapmans rented a cottage at Perranporth in Cornwall. Winnie was a delicate child who as an infant suffered from a 'weak chest'. During one severe illness she was placed in an oxygen tent and for a time was not expected to survive. The sea air and exercise of the Perranporth holidays were of great benefit to her health and, ironically, she outlived her brother and both of her sisters. When the family set off for Perranporth in the summer of 1915 Winnie, aged sixteen, was guarding a secret. Hidden amongst her most treasured possessions was a tiny white envelope containing a single lock of Ivor Gurney's hair. Upon it she had written in pencil: 'My Dearest Ivor's Curl'.

1

TRAINING FOR WAR

February 1915–May 1916

*Gurney's battalion moved from Gloucester,
first to Northampton and then, in April 1915,
to Chelmsford, from where they made seventeen-
mile route marches to Epping to work on the
defensive trench system for outer London.*

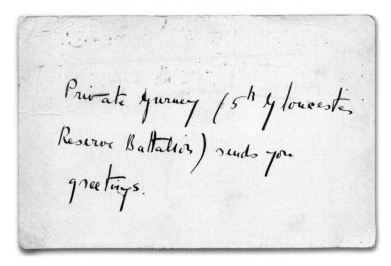

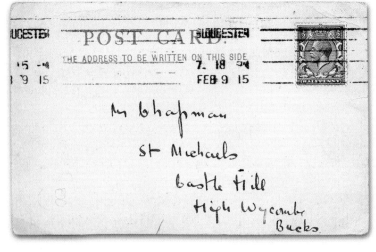

Postcard to Edward Chapman from Gloucester, dated 9 Feb 1915

February 1915 (KT)

Pte I B Gurney
B Company
2nd 5th Glosters
Northampton

My Dear Chapmen

Well, life is distinctly harder here than at Gloucester. 1st parade 7–7.45 Physical Drill. 2nd 9–12.45 Drill, 2–4.30 Drill. Hard work too, but I hang on and hope for the best. I think I shall come through. If it tires me, it tires the other recruits also and so I don't care.

I was going to send my billet address, but that is forbidden, and besides I did not like my first billet and have now changed it. You may expect an army biscuit by post soon. Personally I rather like them, and though they are terrifically hard, hot tea alters that.

I hope everybody is well and out of bed, and – oh yes! Did Arthur get his Sherlock Holmes, and has he liked them? I could not find the one supposed to be left at home.

How is the ping-pong, and the hockey, and Moses and all? My thoughts go back to High Wycombe and the ping-pong tournaments 'and all' with pleasure, and the conviction that I should not be as well now if it were not for that.

I think there is no danger of my breaking down, and a large prospect of my becoming much better, thank the Lord, and paid a bob a day for it, too!

The chaps at my billet (3) are very nice and we ought to have some good evenings together. How is Mr Ketchlee? Tell him to advertise for the Lost Tribes in the Agony column of *The Times*. If the Germans answer it, then of course his theory is wrong.

Goodbye

Your affectionate friend
Ivor Gurney

9 March 1915 (P)

Pte Ivor Gurney
6 Platoon
B Company
2nd 5th Glosters
Northampton

My Dear Chapmen

I should have replied to that P.C. but never got it. Some of my things have gone astray to a man in this Company named J. Gurney, and he forgot to let me have it. I have not yet thanked you for the writing case – which is charming, nor the pipe lighter, which is very useful on a march; especially in a wind.

I hope the family is all right now and jolly and revelling in ping-pong tournaments galore. I am afraid you will not see me this side of the war. Leave is very difficult to get, and as I was such a short time at home it must be spent there; if I get any at all. Tomorrow the foreign service men do their firing; those who pass the tests may be at the front any time soon. Our first 5th (of which we are the reserve) may go at any time, and reserves are not kept waiting long in *this* war.

Our rifles are of Japanese make, but some others are to be served out for firing – the Lee-Enfield type.

No, I am not ill. Indeed they tell me I look much better; and, indeed, I must be pretty strong for a neurastheniac.

Yesterday I was on from 8.15–12.15, 3–5.30, 7.15–10 and then we had an alarm and turned out at 11 not to get back till 2.15.

The ordinary day is

6.45–7.30

8.45–12.30

2.00–4.30

This I do and am never very tired, though during last night's alarm I marched in a sort of dream, but this fatigue was healthy and not nervous exhaustion. The food has been wretched, but now is better. Half my money has gone on extra food, chiefly meat, a substance considered in the Army to be composed entirely of fat, bone and gristle. I buy bully beef when it becomes too annoying. We may leave here for Chelmsford any day; and from Chelmsford perhaps – who knows? – to the Dardanelles. There are rumours . . .

Well, this is all about myself, but the details about Army life are from the inside, and, chiefly, about the inside. I do not at all forget you – Pa and Ma, Kitty, Winnie and the exuberant Mickie. Not by no means. But rifles, boots, buttons, need cleaning; coats need rolling, clothes brushing; and there are night operations, street pickets, fire pickets, and guards to be done.

May you all be happy and healthy and wealthy and wise – more so every day. Good-bye to all of you. Easter is near; and after then, I am no more organist of

Christ Church – my official tie to High Wycombe will be gone, and there will be left that unofficial one of being your friend.

Yours affectionately
Ivor

On back of envelope: Would you like a hay band or a straw – ? I've finished with mine.[1]

POSTCARD addressed to Mr Chapman, St Michael's, etc., Dated: 8 April 1915.

I got your letter yesterday morning. It was such a pity. I should very much have liked to have seen you again – but there is a chance next week. I believe – *believe* mind, that we go to Epping Forest on Friday.

IBG

POSTCARD addressed to Mrs Chapman, St Michael's, etc., Dated: 21 April 1915.

Dear Comtesse

Thank you for your nice letter. As for arrangements, they must be hopelessly vague. We are reported to be leaving here either on Sat: or Monday. I heard that

[1] At an earlier time, country men unfamiliar with the 'left, right' of marching orders were reputedly given a hay band to tie round one leg and a straw band for the other. The drill instructor could then call out 'hay, straw' instead of 'left, right'.

the Captain told our platoon so today fairly definitely. If it is true (and I think it is) we return to Chelmsford, another 17 miles! But nothing – nothing is certain, but uncertainty.

IBG

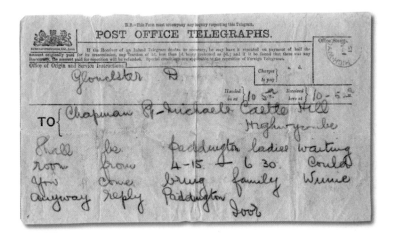

POST OFFICE TELEGRAM

Addressed: Chapman, St Michael's, Castle Hill, High Wycombe
Dated: 17 May 1915

Message: Shall be Paddington ladies waiting room from 4.15–6.30. Could you come bring family Winnie anyway Reply Paddington Ivor

June 1915 (KT)

Pte Gurney
B Company, 2nd 5th Glosters
Chelmsford, Essex

Dear Old Winnie

Thank you for your letter, and Dear Comtesse, thank you for the cake, which is *good*, and dear Micky, thank you also for *your* letter.

I am sorry you poor creatures that there has been such a pestilence and famine among you. And so unseasonable a thing as rheumatism; which should go with winter and plum puddings. I am writing this near Galley wood outside Chelmsford. We are on what is called anti-aircraft picket. That is – we are on the lookout for Zeppelins etc. And at this time it should be exciting enough. We get out about 7 p.m. and stay till 6 a.m. In fine weather it is very good fun; both sunset and dawn are beautiful, and there is only an hour's guard each.

This will be my last till next Sunday.

Bayonet practice is over now, and we ought to have more firing soon.

How is Arthur getting on at cricket? Good scores and hat tricks I hope.

We are leaving here soon I believe, for somewhere near Epping perhaps.

Well goodbye, Winnie dear, and I hope the toothache is quite well now, and Daddie's rheumatics.

Love to Everybody and no rheumatism or crocking up of any kind.

Yours affectionately
Ivor

Stars in a Dark Night

June 1915 (KT)

My Dear Winnie

I wonder how you too are getting on, you poor imp of misery. (This is a letter to a lady.) It is the patriotic duty of every English woman to wear a pack now, and I don't feel disposed to write politely to anyone who doesn't – and 60 lbs at least in weight. But blessings on thee. Thou art a blithesome thing, God wot. Would that it had been possible to have taught thy nimble finger the divine Beethoven, but the gods willed otherwise.

I suppose you are looking forward to Perranporth and to see the great Atlantic rollers in a perpetual surge and attack on our England. My spirit will be with you there, chasing the bunnies or quietly watching the 'sunshot palaces high' and breathing contentment with the common air. This seems to be a frightfully high faluting letter; but you will understand it, and it is such a restful thing, to high-falute. Many of our occupations are 'so low, my dear'. But this morning I sat hidden behind a table, on my beam-ends and had a high old time learning the Morse alphabet and reading the paper. This afternoon, now at this moment, was to be given to us as a time of peace, as we are to be out all night, but They (a malison on them!) could not let us be, and ordained a hut-inspection, and of kits etc. But Private Gurney did espy the orderly corporal in the next hut, and got him outside straightway to listen at the window; whence he is now writing letters in a wood a mile away from camp – even this to his

amiable correspondent, Mistress Winfred Chapman, to whom he sends his love and best wishes.
Goodbye

Yours affectionately
Ivor B.

June 1915 (KT)

To the Paleface Chief Arthur

Glass-eyes, the player on instruments, sends thee greeting.

Prays the Great White Chief for thy welfare and desires to know the state of thy health. Announces that he has 4 or 5 loaded blanks which may arrive at Chief Arthur's wigwam at any moment, should an insurrection headed by Smith, the Rushes By[2] (the henpecked medicine man) or any such washout (keep that dark though, destroy the missive). But really old man, are you all right now? Body, soul and spirit, and between the cracks?

Here there are no more blizzards, but Spring with the sweetest smiles, and so I hope you are cricketing – on the hearth or elsewhere.

But I am sure you stood what you had to pluckily as befits an Englishman. Someday we will hunt together on Keep Hill, and gather many scalps to hang round our umbrellas. Till then,

Farewell and Greetings.

Yours affectionately
Ivor

[2] The Reverend Rushby-Smith, vicar of Christ Church, High Wycombe. Mrs Rushby-Smith was the choir mistress.

June 1915 (KT)   Chelmsford, Essex
                                                       1915

My Dear Comtesse

I am very sorry, but everything has turned out a failure.
On the last two Saturdays I have been inoculated and on
guard, and the few hours I hoped for either yesterday or
today have not been granted. I should have written
before; but camp has been very hard, and when there
was any spare time it was spent on the flat of my back.
Reveille 5 Breakfast 6.30 Dinner 1.30 Tea 4.30–5.0,
and on all the time between those hours!

I am sorry not to have written, but always hoped to
be able to let you know I was able to get a Saturday
pass. Hope you will all enjoy Perran.

Yours affectionately
Ivor

June 1915 (KT)

My Dear Old Winnie

Bless you my child; yours was a nice letter for a war
weary son of a gun to get.

I hope you will get your reward at Perran, and play
endless exciting games of tennis; and have delightful
cool – but not chilly – bathes, generally enjoying
yourself as you deserve.

Well, it doesn't look much like seeing you for some
ages yet. Before this week 1 man a company per week

was *supposed* to go. This week leave is again violently smitten on the head (a frequent occurrence with us) and may have succumbed to its injuries.

My fairy-godmother is most frightfully slack. Perhaps she is after the vote on Proportional Representation or summat new-fangled. I am, I hope I may say – a just man, a long-suffering and humble servant; (Don't this sound like Lloyd George) but even fairy-godmothers can get it in the neck. And this particular one has been asking for it for a pretty long time.

When will the days of peace and plenty and beaucoup ping pong once again return? Alack, man knoweth not. Nor young women either, in spite of their growing up, putting their hair up, putting on frills, and fine raiment, and generally startling and upsetting their humble adorers – of whom I am

(Very affectionately)
one of the wormiest and most enthralled
Ivor

29 June 1915 (P)   Pte Gurney
                                                    B Company
                                              2nd 5th Glosters
                                            Wintry Farm, Camp
                                                Epping, Essex

My Dear Chapmen

We have been here in camp just over a week, and the whole time has been a rush from 5 o'clock reveillé to 9.45 Lights out. The chief thing is attacks and all sorts of company and brigade actions; this is why we have come into camp. The roads are horrid, bristly with shingle and pebbles which raise blisters in record time. For breakfast we have as a rule bacon; for dinner either what they call shackles (stewed meat) or roast meat; for tea, bread, margarine, jam, and 'tea', made in the same dixie as the shackles – very different in every way to the dainty meal held about the same time at St Michael's High Wycombe. No oatcake, no scones; likewise no ping-pong. If you would like to see in camp, one is allowed to bring people in on Sundays, when the camp deletes as much of its grease as possible, ameliorates its language, and relaxes the stern visage of war.

The Bucks, the Oxford and Bucks, the Glosters, the Berks and a few Engineers and RAMC are all here-abouts, and all affable to visitors.

Camp open from 3–9.

Has Arthur made any great scores lately? And what has Winnie done? Micky I suppose is just as naughty and nice as ever, all reared on the bounteous provision prepared by the Comtesse and made possible by the arduous exertions of the Count.

Our first reinforcements have gone – three days ago, and our second are ready to go; and so the Brigade gradually dribbles out to the Front.

Well, good bye, all you dear creatures in Buckinghamshire. Oh, does anyone want an exciting book about Scotland? *The New Road* by Neil Munro would suit.

Good bye

Your affectionate friend
Ivor Gurney

July 1915 (KT)   Pte Gurney
                                                  6 Platoon,
                                                  2nd 5th Glosters
                                                  Epping

My Dear Comtesse

I am so sorry that you have had so wretched a time
at so unprofitable a game. It is hard lines on one
who would like to live life to be cooped up in bed
and see the clouds drift and do nothing and be nothing
of importance.

Of course I forgive the lecture. It was deserved,
though not so much as you think perhaps. The 'nice
long evenings' are occasionally filled up by army
duties, such as guard, street picket, night operations,
fatigue. And last Monday we marched 17 miles,
hunted for billets, and at 7.30, when I was about to
go in, I was collared for duty and got two hours sleep,
and on duty all next day. Besides, unlike yourself I
hate writing.

That 17 miles was with the pack – that is, about 40
lbs to carry.

We shall be here till Monday week, but whether I
can get leave or no is doubtful. Of course I do not
mean my 48 hours leave which would be spent in
Gloucester – but leave till 12 at night. Not this
Saturday anyway, but perhaps next. On Sunday I am
on guard. Please thank Micky for her letter. It was
just like the dear rascal, and I wish I were back to
lose to Arthur and Winifred Emma the champion
once again.

I wish you all were not so good to me. I like my

friends to be willing to give to me in proportion to what myself would give, and you are all too generous in affection and otherwise.

Hoping you are better now, with love to all

I remain

Your affectionate
Ivor Gurney

POSTCARD to 'Messrs Chapman' from Epping, dated 9th July, 1915.

Message reads:
'Why did they take Them
or
The Drunken Recruiting Officer'

August 1915 (KT)   Pte Gurney
                                    B Company
                                    2nd 5th Glosters
                                    Chelmsford
                                    Essex

My Dear Winifreda

Thank you for the P.C. and your letter to which I never replied, miserable sinner that I am! Bless you my child for your friendship and thoughts of me. Now they have put me in our new brass band – on second-hand instruments – I shall have more time and in all probability become fat and lazy. ('Fat and well-liking' the Psalmist says).

I hope all you dear creatures are happy and dirty down at Perran. Why have colds? Why have minor ailments? What use are they? What cash value do they represent? What relation do they bear toward the Eternal Verities? (Carlyle, whom some day you will read).

My landlady here curiously enough stayed at Perranporth years and years ago; she loves it, and likes to speak of it.

She is an individual old girl, with a mind of her own, and very kind.

I was sorry not to see you before you went, especially as it is probably the last chance. I have had no leave for about 14 weeks, and no half-day leave since I saw you all. Kitchener has now seen and passed us. We are to be ready to take our places when wanted, and so the 5 days leave preliminary to going abroad has just started, and the first batch went today. I must at least see the

The Chapmans' holiday cottage at Perranporth, Cornwall.
A watercolour by G.F. Beckett

Winnie, Micky, a friend, and the Chapman family pet, Barry, on the beach at Perranporth

Comte at Paddington when my time comes, which may be in about 3 weeks time.

Don't get drowned, or sucked down by shifting sands, or get battered to bits by those huge Atlantic rollers. How are the trout?[3]

I hope to see you all again one day, sound in body and mind, and to give you all a hundred runs and beat you, or 49 points out of 50 at ping-pong and beat you; you half-Gaelic rapscallions!

Good bye, Winnie dear, and increase in wisdom, stature and health, and tell me all about yourself when you write. No polite inquiries!

Yours affectionately
Ivor

August 1915 (KT)   Pte Gurney
                                               B Company
                                        2nd 5th Glosters
                                             Chelmsford
                                                  Essex

My Dear Comtesse

I am sorry that worries pursue you even down in Cornwall, and that the poor kids are not up to the mark. Perhaps it is all right now, and the sun is shining.

[3] Gurney's detailed knowledge of Perranporth suggests that he had stayed there with the Chapmans in the summer of 1914.

St Michael's on the right

Why do you suppose that when you do not get a letter, I am 'cross'? Well, it is an old trick now, and a legitimate one, though doubtfully useful as you must realise that I don't take fits of *that* kind, anyhow.

I am glad to be able to tell you – that my mind is gradually becoming more sane and more happy. It is hard work, but now [that] I realise to the full that it is chiefly my mind at fault, I push on that way; and feel more hopeful. But please don't praise me for my courage! It is my only chance of happiness and health.

You won't mind this bit of self-analysis I hope? It is better to do very little of it, though.

Don't overwork yourself and spoil your holiday; it is better and nobler by far to worry over other people than yourself, but why do either?

Have you got Browning at all? The second volume of Everyman is excellent; or did I give you that little red-covered volume? That is good too. You ought to get Wordsworth in that edition; it is first rate.

What must the sea look like? The sea – unbroken in force by any barrier for thousands of miles! What free grace and careless glory must show itself in such unhampered movements. Well, probably (by statistics and ordinary reckoning) I myself may take joy in it someday; when this tyranny is overpast.

They have made a brass band now, and for the present put me in it; on a [*sic*] instrument called the Baryton – a bass cornet-affair. I like it, though my lips are too thick ever to do it justice, perhaps. Still, practice may put that right.

Now go I to bathe in the Chelmer; not an imposing river; nothing of the 'rude imperious surge' about it.

Good luck!

Yours affectionately
Ivor

15 September 1915 (P)

PteGurney
B Company
2nd 5th Glosters
Chelmsford
Essex

My Dear Creatures

It was good-as-gold of you to send me such a parcel of good things. Never have I felt such a sensation of

Officers of the Great Western Railway Goods Department

Supplement to "GREAT WESTERN RAILWAY MAGAZINE" January 1921   PHILIP REID, FLEET ST, LONDON. E

overwhelming luxury and surprise of riches since (alas! Many years agone; lang syne) I bought a penny lucky bag and discovered a real wooden monkey on a real wooden stick. The air cushion is not at present useful to me, but if we have to sleep out it will be a blessing unparalleled. The tin will do for baccy, stamps, stray sovereigns, maggots and beetles, small photos.[4] What the handkerchiefs will do for is better left out. Praps some day I may find the need for soap.

I wrote a p.c. to Mr Chapman about a week ago, telling him that I should be in London at a certain time. Two days after I remembered that the address on the p.c. was Mr Chapman – Goods Manager. So that may have been the reason I did not see him. Perhaps he lost his post through the G.M.'s jealousy and so has left you down at Perranporth to live on rabbits till he can scheme some money or other. Perhaps he's dead of grief, all through an unfortunate slip. I'm very sorry if this is so; he was a man who, though enthusiasm would be out of place, was not altogether bad: he was not as black at some points as others. His chief use was to excuse, by the display of his imperfections, any tendency to gaucherie or villainy in his children. And a good excuse it was for them, on almost anything.

(Just for sentiment's sake I will light up, and accompany this letter with Winnie's etceteras pipe and baccy. Puff, puff! Thank you!).

The foregoing is written in pencil; the remainder, following a break in time, in ink.

---

[4] It was a small, flat tin of Bournville Cocoa, measuring 2½in x 1¾in x ⅝in.

I am very sorry to have left this letter for so long. It was very wrong when there was [*sic*] so many nice presents to thank you for. They are all in use, save only the cushion, or rather pillow, for which, thank Goodness, no occasion for use has yet arisen.

I am afraid that your visit to Perranporth is drawing to an end. But you must draw cold comfort from the fact that High Wycombe is a very nice place to live in. Compare it with any London suburb.

My best friend has just got a D.S.M.[5] and has been recommended for a commission, but his nerves are pretty shaky. When we are to go, no one knows, but from rumours it is not likely to be just yet. But what are rumours worth?

[5] F.W. Harvey, and it was a D.C.M. (Distinguished Conduct Medal). The citation reads: '2371 Lance-Corpl. F.W. Harvey, 1/5th Gloucestershire R. (T.F.) – for conspicuous gallantry on the night of Aug. 3–4, 1915, near Hebuterne, when, with a patrol, he and another non-commissioned officer went out to reconnoitre in the direction of a suspected listening-post. In advancing they encountered the hostile post, evidently covering a working party in the rear. Corporal Knight at once shot one of the enemy, and, with Lance-Corporal Harvey, rushed the post, shooting two others, and, assistance arriving, the enemy fled. Lance-Corporal Harvey pursued, felling one of the retreating Germans with a bludgeon. He siezed him, but, finding his revolver empty and the enemy having opened fire, he was called back by Corporal Knight, and the prisoner escaped. Three Germans were killed, and their rifles and a Mauser pistol were brought in. The patrol had no loss.' Both Will Harvey and Raymond Knight were commissioned on 15 October 1915; Knight was killed on the Somme in July 1916, and is commemorated in a memorial plaque on the wall of Gloucester Cathedral cloisters, to the right of the Chapter House door.

I should like a game of ping-pong very much: it would appeal to me more than forming fours or other such manifestations of military glory.

My 5 days leave happened about a week ago, more than a week in fact; and the beauty of my own county astounded and enchanted me more than ever. As a friend of mine has lately written –

> 'I'm homesick for my hills again,
> My hills again!
> To see above the Severn plain
> Unscabbarded against the sky
> The blue high blade of Cotswold lie;
> And giant clouds go royally
> By jagged Malvern with a train of shadows.'[6]

Isn't it exquisite?

Good bye all you unfortunate people who weren't born there!

Yours affectionately
Ivor

---

[6] The first stanza of 'In Flanders' by F.W. Harvey, written whilst at Ploegsteert ('Plug Street'), Belgium, before his transfer to France. Gurney made a song-setting of the poem in 1916.

Stars in a Dark Night

September 1915 (AB)   Pte Gurney
                                    Band D Company
                                              etc

My Dear Comtesse

I wonder how you like High Wycombe now? The change from Perranporth must be great, but let it not blind you to the merits of High Wycombe, which are many.

Today is bright and bracing, and after flat and featureless Essex, Bucks would be Beauty personified. Walk you straight round Castle Hill and be glad of it. I hope you are pretty well and cheery after your long holiday – it was a long one you know; and you must not have wasted money by not feeling a jolly sight better.

You are quite wrong about my not wanting letters. I like them better than for years I have (a sure sign of improving health), and am glad of them. But I *don't* like wee bits from R.M. or A.E. Benson, and sentimental 'Weltmüthings'[7] to give you a Teutonism. They insult God and Man, either by refusing to see the truth, or insisting on unimportant platitudes. I like letters to be about people who write them. 'A healthy egotism' as our German friends would say. There is a distinct possibility that we shall not go abroad till March, which will make the chances of getting through all right quite large.

My mind gradually tranquillises itself, and more and more I see what a splendid teacher Wordsworth is for all sorts of men. When I can lie quite still in joy by the side of some stream or in a meadow for an hour or

---

[7] A made-up word, probably meaning 'musings about the world'.

more, then music will come easily and well. Not till then. Happiness is in ourselves, and until this is a platitude to be smiled at for its obviousness, it is not possible for sensitive people to be happy. Come and let's be – together. At present, it is probable that I am in front.

I find I have been preaching. Sorry! But it is as much for myself as you.

But . . . does that make it any more excusable? I wonder . . .

Your affectionately
Ivor

Oh, Mr Smith[8] has not replied to my letter. The one before was curt. Is this due to my attitude on Prophesy? Have you the Everyman *Century of Essays?* If so, did I give it to you? If not, *please* let me have it.

September 1915 (AB)

My Dear Kids

How's hockey? How's dogs? How's football? How's Keep Hill?

I would very much like to share all these with you, but Lord Kitchener won't let me. Herbert Horatio Has the Hump. But really: Essex is a flat and unsatisfactory place, and now Autumn is in the air I remember High Wycombe, and how I went down there just about this

---

[8] The Reverend Rushby-Smith.

time last year, and discovered a family which liked Bach and whose presents I am now loaded with. I take baccy from a magnificent sterling silver pouch-thing, light up a splendid Spring Model pipe, and recline on a lovely Latest Style air-cushion, carefully dusting my trousers with an exquisite handkerchief embroidered (as is the cushion) with my name, and am ready to sneeze in the most gentlemanly fashion into the most lady-like handkerchiefs. Is Winnie going back to School? What will Kitty do? Is Arthur going to take a commission? Is Micky allowed to associate with other more respectable children?

How's dad? with whom I used to settle the fate of Europe and the Universe with my feet pointing upwards to the skies, as the hymn says.

Mr Jack White is in the Naval Air service now, and has made trips into the empyrean (Gotcher!)

Oh, dear! but how sick we are of the army; and how we watch the placards for any indication of a near end to the war. Things are rosy just at present, rosier than they were, anyhow. It's Sunday, today, and were things different from what they are, I might be looking forward to clutching hold of about 6 pairs of hands and trying not to break my neck, and look affable! Do you remember how the Gadarene swine used to run down the quarry at Keep Hill? Well, one day again perhaps . . .

Good bye everybody

Your affectionate friend
Ivor

October 1915 (AB)

My Dear Micky

I hope you have been doing no very naughty things lately, you imp of iniquity, you! How many times have you fallen in, and upset the whole household for clean clothes? How many dogs have you worried, you extreme example of wilful perversity? How many cats? children? Mothers? Sisters? Brothers? Aunts?

But indeed, I may be quite sure that it will take more than a European war, and a wetting to damp your spirits and stop you dancing. Go on then, be naughty and get muddy. It is not I that have to set things straight. They may scold, but I am far enough away not to mind so much, and all I want is a letter about it, and kisses at the end.

Draw me a picture, lady-artist. Make me a song. Play tricks – and – naughtiness all the day long.

Yours affectionately
Ivor B

POSTCARD

To Mrs Chapman, St Michael's, High Wycombe, Bucks'
Dated by postmark: 22 October 1915.

Sorry not to have answered your letters, but ever since Monday we have been out on manoeuvres; and civilisation a thing unknown.

I have made application for Sunday leave, but shall

not know till then whether I shall get it. If you knew what a time we have had this past 3 weeks you would not suspect any sane person of not wishing to get anywhere else. But I'm afraid you'll have to pay for it. IBG

October 1915 (KT)
Pte Gurney
Band. D. Co. 2/5 Glosters
Chelmsford

My Dear Comte (de Tilda) = title of female succession

The Comtesse your gracious consort has written me a charming letter all about herself (and myself), but happens to mention that you would like a letter from me; and as it is rather important to me to keep in with you, I take the hint, though there is not much to say.

There was no train from London that night, and so after sleeping for an hour or two at a Soldiers and Sailors home – a most comfy 3d doss – I went down to prison on the paper train at 5 a.m.

When we (for there were other daredevils besides myself) handed our passes in, the following dramatic scene occurred – from the play *An Escape from Gehenna*.

Act I   Hurried evasion
Act II   High Wycombe
Act III   Doss house in London slums
Act IV   Handing the Pass In

Scene: Quarter-Guard Room
(Enter two men of doubtful mien and hangdog air)

1st Guard	Hullo!
1st Criminal	Ah do! Where's the Sergeant?
1st Guard	There.
1st Criminal	Thanks . . . Sorry, Sergeant, to wake you up. Here they are.
Sergeant	(Grunt . . . Grunt . . . Grunt . . .) 'Ere, wot's this?
1st Criminal	
2nd Crim:	Wot's Wot?
Sergeant	This! Wot's this? These are midnight passes.
1st Criminal	Ah, yes . . . most unfortunate. *Most* unfortunate. Somehow or other there didn't happen to be a train after 8.30. They must have taken 'em off. Bit rotten, wasn't it . . . We didn't mean to disturb you. Very sorry. Won't do it again. Quite a mistake.
Sergeant	Ah . . . Well, you just get off into your billets at once. There 'ud be a blushing row if anybody seen you.
1st Crim	
2nd "	Oh yes . . . thanks, Sergeant. Good morning

Exeunt

Act V   has not yet come, and doesn't look like it.

It was good to get back to St Mike's again, bless it, and feel free and golopshus once again.

We went out on a brigade stunt, and got a dinner of bone splinters and hot water at 4 o'clock next day; so

83

the impression of cloistral peace was heightened by contrast. Curious that a rotten liver should be able to spoil everything save only memories . . .

The Comtesse says you are in Wales, and have not yet seen the miracle-working gent who may be able to recall me, like Orpheus, from Hell.[9] That doesn't affect me much . . . I do not dare to hope much for fear. . . .

But if it is real, and not phantasmal and only a rosy dream, let the proof be forthcoming not too late. I may be snatched away of a sudden into some remote outlandish place outside England, but that is not immediately likely, though there are rumours.

I might also say that if there is another place, Cridlan, that analyst etc. from Stevens [*sic*] Jammery[10] would be delighted to get it, and would if necessary get references from his uncles. He would certainly be very useful. Well, that's all about that for — FOR THE PRESENT I hope.

Oh, but this is a grey unuseful unbeautiful waste, this Essex. No suns, etc, no colours. No beechy hills, no downs, no nothing, no kids to play with, no free cigarettes, no ping-pong. No something that gives romance and mystery to ordinary trees and hedges and houses in more fortunate parts. If ever I come to write music some of it will be around Totteridge, Keep Hill, and the Macbeth-like wood that lies beyond it to the south. Some of it also around the homelife which is so strong and sweet a stimulant to any sound art.

But this is rather gassy. Get me out of this. Let me

---

[9] Edward Chapman was attempting to secure a job in railway transport with the Great Western Railway for Gurney.
[10] Stephens Jam Factory in Gloucester.

know that I shall still be doing war-duty with a practical certainty of being some day able to do all that lies in me, some day, for the honour of England; which is very dear to me. Indeed, if I could feel certain that there never would be anything in me really worth the showing in music, the first thing I'd do would be to volunteer where they wanted me most. Though on that point even, I believe that the Railway Transport, if there is a chance to rise, will give me a fair run.

Please forgive this egotistical letter, but I can write no others that are not washy platitudes.

Yours affectionately
Ivor Gurney

December 1915 (P)   Pte Gurney
2/5 Glosters
Chelmsford

My Dear Comtesse

I thoroughly expected to be with you today, but we are on Brigade duties, and have had so many extra things to do that I did not think it worth while to apply – rightly, as it turned out. But either next Saturday or Sunday will do I think. Probably Saturday – as I could stay till 10, if there is a train then. You say it is a pleasure to see me. I suppose it is difficult for a person outside the Army to know what a delight the mere being absent from quarters is. And when the return is to delicate food, white tablecloths, large, or largish rooms, and such company as I can get at High Wycombe, then the feeling lasts as much as a week, and one is able to stand a whole 7 days without too much remembering the feeling of utter futility and waste of time that is the average thought of any educated man in the Army life. I am not at all sure that we shall not be glad to get abroad – glad for a time anyhow; and that seems to be coming not long after Xmas.

Thank you, Madam; the food is better now. Indeed, I have left quite a lot lately. It is to be hoped your progeny (there's an expression to be applied to such children!) are either well or on the mend now.

As for winter trees – I believe, never are they so beautiful as now. Never are afterglows so far beyond words to describe as in Winter. And never is teatime so lovely a thing to be looked forward to – or regretted most in the Army.

But I don't grumble. My health improves all the time. I am fit for double as much as when I joined 9 months ago. My mind can escape from itself a little. I think of music with some pleasure, and in another 6 months I ought [to] be able clearly to see my way to such health of mind and body as never before. Why not you, too? It is a question of thought and not overworking and Joy consciously created till the creation becomes habitual and spontaneous. And as for worrying – If the maker of Stars and Waters and Trees does not know his business, I am afraid that there is no one who can teach him.

Good bye, and best of luck. O, I forgot to mention the Railway job. I am afraid it will be very difficult as there are only 612 of us. That is to say only 12 more can leave. But I never worry about possibilities, or hardly ever.

Yours affectionately
Ivor

[On reverse of envelope Gurney has written: Letter and mittens just received Thank you!*]*

December 1915 (KT)   Pte Gurney
etc

My Dear Old People

You'll not have me with you, I fear, just yet. Never mind, I don't care whether its Xmas day or not, you shall have me with you before very long, as we are getting leave in bits. My bit will probably not be very long delayed. I only hope you racketty kids won't be at school when the auspicious occasion ausps.

Remember me in thy down-sitting and thy uprising. At the pinging of the pong, and the rendering on the tinkles. Sing you loud and lustily, and use your windbags bustily; prostrate yourselves every five minutes, reverently murmuring 'I.B.G.', and no doubt something will reward you; though the time be long-distant, and its connection with the act doubtful and hard to trace.

Bless you, my children
(From 60 downwards)

Your affectionate
I.B.G.

December 1915 (KT)

My Dear Old Winnie

I am sorry you have been sick and at such an untactful time of holidays. Perhaps it is all better now. Bless you my child, I hope so. As for the photo, it simply hasn't arrived, and my laziness has prevented me writing to know why.

I hope to see you next Sunday, and it is fairly certain that I shall – or on Saturday.

What a funny Xmas this will be! Away from everything in the way of Children and ping-pong. Anyway, I shall be feeling much better this year than last, and not such a drag on the entertainment as then; for we simply must get up some sort of entertainment in this dead-alive unfortunate hole. Either 4 or 8 of us are plotting how to make believe that Army life may be made jolly about Christmas time. We'll do it, somehow. Unless they stick us on guard, or the extremely military operation of picking up paper. Anyway, I hope you will concentrate all your psychic [*sic*] faculties on having a damgood time then; and remembering me only to pledge me in the quaffing of huge tankards of beer, to the shouts of Waeshael! Let the ancestral hall of St Michael, and its stately keep and barbican echo to the sound.

Stars in a Dark Night

Epic on the Celebration of the Mass of Christ

> Kinkering Kongs
>   Do ping their pongs
> And title-takers
>   Get stomach achers.[11]

Tell tales all round again. Put your hand on each others backs, and count the shivers. Judge each ghost tale, not only by the frequency of the shivers but also by their duration and wobblyness.
Good bye dear and best wishes

Yours affectionately
Ivor

POSTCARD with photograph of the 2nd 5th Battalion Gloucester Regiment band in 1915, showing Gurney in the rear rank, fourth from the right.

Addressed to Messrs Chapman and Co., St Michael's, etc.

Dated: 17 December 1915 (P)

Merry Xmas and don't forget last year's ping-pong and beeeeastly wet,
Likewise especially

I.B.G.

[11] Reference to the hymn beginning 'Conquering Kings their titles take' by John Chandler (1806–76), from the Latin, as in *Hymns Ancient and Modern.*

The 2nd/5th Battalion Gloucester Regiment Band in 1915. Ivor Gurney
is in the rear rank, fourth from right

New Year 1916 (KT)

My Dear Chapmen

Indeed you are darlings of a special sort. The birthday book of my beloved William[12] is charming, and you know what I think of the oatcake and scones you make. But why have you not written in the book?

Where are your birthdays?

I suppose the dangerous looking tin is a footwarmer? O individuals of great price. As for leave, and consequently coming to see you, I knows nowt. Not before Friday week anyhow, as far as I can see.

So please expect me on a visit either next Saturday or Sunday, but this is not certain. The Band has had some rough times lately, and one hardly knows what is going to happen.

But Cheero. Leave cannot be long away; anyway not if the strong rumour is true that we are moving in February. Goodbye everybody.

Dad and the Lad. Mick and the Rest of the Click.

Yours affectionately
Ivor

---

[12] Wordsworth.

New Year 1916 (KT)

My Dear Comtesse

This kindness comes from all of you, but it bears the special mark of Tildaness upon it. Kindness follows me through life, and I can say at least this for myself, that it bewilders me, and makes me shy. But you must be doing these things, I suppose. Thank you very much indeed.

As my letter says, the Family letter, I hope to see you soon and to get an oasis of green in this dreary-same life. But I keep pretty cheery, and have no doubt you are practising the noble art of keeping your pecker up. Anyway, let's all hope you will all keep well and happy in this coming New Year. What would not the end of the war and a week or so at Wycombe mean to me? Nevertheless, we cultivate the habit of slummocking along without worry and smiling at Life. Oatcake is no contemptible help to this, nor Wordsworth either.

Thank you

> *Yours affectionately*
> Ivor

18 February 1916 (P)

My Dear Chapmen

After all, Harvey could not get leave, and so every part of my plan miscarried, and we never met. Well, well; so wags the world. Receive herewith the grateful wherewithal. This is chiefly to let you know that we are nearly certain to be off on Saturday to Tidworth that haunt of devils. If so, it is not so far from Reading – and consequently from the Merry Chapmen. Prepare to receive music and books forthwith.

Yours affectionately
Ivor

On 17th February 1916, the Royal College of Music Union sent a copy of a printed circular to Gurney:

Dear Mr Gurney,

It has been brought to the notice of the R.C.M. Union General Committee that some of the Members who are on Active Service may have experienced difficulties in arranging for the maintenance of their professional musical interests during their enforced absence, and may be glad to know where to apply in the event of their wanting a temporary teacher for their pupils, a reliable deputy to take over a position, or a responsible representative to gather any royalties from publishers which may accrue.

It has therefore been suggested that it might be desirable to form a Sub-Committee of the R.C.M. Union for this purpose, but before any definite steps are taken the General Committee has requested us to enquire into the matter, and to ascertain the views of Members on Active Service. It will be of the greatest help to us if you will kindly let us know at your earliest convenience what your views are, and whether such a scheme would be of any service to you personally. Replies should be sent to the Hon. Secretary (MISS MARION SCOTT) at the above address.

Yours faithfully,

Marion M. Scott   Harold Samuel
Mabel Saumarez Smith   Harold E.Darke[13]

Gurney's reply is on the reverse of the above circular :

Dear Committee

I have experienced no great difficulty in arranging for the maintenance of my professional musical interests, for at the best they were only slightly more than nil. As for requiring a temporary teacher, you could serve me little in this, but for any temporary pupils – at half a guinea a lesson of 20 minutes – I should feel most grateful. Your remark about collecting royalties happens merely to be ironic; and so does not give me anything like the pleasure the other offer does – that offer to provide a reasonable deputy for my position.

My position is at present that of a private in the 2/5 battalion of the Gloucesters, who are about to move to huts on Salisbury plain. Any deputy, trustworthy or otherwise, would be most gratefully welcomed, and fulsomely flattered, receive all my military decorations, and valuable insight into the best methods of mud-cleaning with vocal accompaniment.

Yours truly   Ivor Gurney

[13] GA: G.61.144.

Stars in a Dark Night

*On Saturday 19th February 1916, the men of Gurney's
battalion were taken by train to Tidworth, from where they
marched through heavy snow to Park House Camp on
Salisbury Plain. They arrived to find that there were no
beds, fires or electric lights. The men slept on the bare floor
through a bitterly cold night of wind and snow.*

March 1916 (KT)

Pte Gurney
D Co. 2/5 Glosters
Park House Camp
Salisbury

My Dear Comtesse

I was sorry to receive so sad a letter from you. One does
not like to think of one's friends suffering, and for your
complaint, I have of course a particular feeling. I hope
that you are not eating too little; that is worse than
eating too much by far.

Yes, we have left Chelmsford all right, we did so a
fortnight ago; and have been literally freezing ever
since. It *has* been cold, and most of us are wheezing
and coughing when we are not standing at 'shun or
other impossible situations. I might mention, madam,
that should you – I say, if you *should* happen to send a
parcel of eatables, it would not be wasted. Also, if you
could, would you get me another stopper for the air-
cushion; the original stopper has got lost, and the poor
cushion lies useless in my valise.

I hope all the kids are well and happy, occasionally
playing ping-pong as a sort of sacramental
remembrance of IBG. And E. Chapman, who will

receive the most tremendous licking at chess next time we meet – with p—R4 K Kt to B3, K, B to Q B5 etc.

I think we are not very far from going now. A man from the brigade office – who may know nothing says three weeks. I just dodder on and worry as little as my mind will let me.

This is a pretty place, far better than we expected, about 3 miles from Tidworth, almost in Hants. And Huts are far away better than tents. There is a stove going all day to toast things by, and make things look more cheerful, and the men are noisy and happy – they are bellowing popular songs, in a robust but sentimental fashion – a good lot of chaps. Good-bye everybody, and cheer up, ma Comtesse. Always eat a good breakfast, a rule that I live up to now with considerable success. Your description of the concert made me wish a little for music, but not much as yet. Good bye Love to everybody

Yours affectionately
Ivor

POSTCARD from Park House Camp, Salisbury Plain.
Postmark dated 16 March 1916.
To: Messrs Chapman, St Michael's, etc.

Thank you everybody. Letter coming. Meanwhile, please send Davies *Foliage*, and please order R. Bridges' *Poems* in that shilling edition, like the one you keep for me. I think I might set one or two, and must have paper covers. And so, cheero – or Ipsi Pris, as we say.

Ivor

Stars in a Dark Night

20 March 1916 (P)

Pte Gurney
D Co 2/5 Glosters
Park House Camp
Salisbury

My Dear Chapmen

Your parcel was very acceptable to a poor stranded mariner, marooned far from comfortable chairs and hot oatcake and scones; perishing cold, but among men whose cheerfulness not even the devil could daunt, and so, not complaining more than they of my lot.

We don't write many letters here. For myself, I hate the Army so much, and all the worrying little muckings-about fash me so, that I spend the evenings trying to forget all about it. There is firing going on now; I fired the preliminary course, but developed a bad cold, and a cattarh that kept me in continual galvanic movement, no doubt amusing to others, but annoying to myself. But it is merely impossible not to blame oneself in some measure for being unhappy among such men as these. Their vitality is marvellous, their spirits high and continually high.

I am sorry the poor Comtesse has not been well. If good works and a generous heart might make health and happiness, or had anything to do with the distribution of felicity, she should do very well, but alas! it has little to do with me. I make her a present of our little Regulars back-badge, which we are extremely proud of, are to be allowed to wear, and to me are very pretty. More shall follow when it is possible to obtain them.

Thank you kindly for the book which is nearly finished, and then shall be returned, for my book-accommodation is limited, and would do better with you. Thank you very much for the cushion, but is the other one, my name worked thereon, to be wasted for a valve? Nay!

Goodbye, my dears, and bless you all, and again thank you for your cheering letters, like stars in a dark night. Winnie and Micky shall have letters soon. Greeting to the Arch-Power Ted, though he *did* beat me at chess! Yet will I be revenged – revenged.

Yours affectionately
Ivor

*POSTCARD from Park House Camp, Salisbury Plain.
Postmark dated 20 March 1916.
To: Mrs Chapman, St Michael's, etc.*

I forgot to ask you – will you please send me Davies *Foliage* – or whatever it's name is – the green covered book. And please send those R.C.M. Magazines to Mr Watson, 46 Juer Street, Battersea, London S.W.

> My feet – the mud doth stick 'em.
>   Would I were in High Wycombe!
> In divers muds and mucks
>   Worse by far than Bucks.

(unsigned)

*   *   *   *

*In mid-April 1916 Gurney returned to Gloucester on
five days leave, one of which he described in a letter to
Marion Scott,[14] written when he returned to Park House
Camp:*

[. . .] On the Tuesday, the second of the five [probably
18th April], I breakfasted deliciously late, and after
lounging about in a most unmilitary manner with
The Times and *Daily News* I completed my toilet, got
my bike and went down the noblest road I know –
the Gloucester–Malvern road, where all the telegraph
poles are down and great trees lying stricken and low
forever. Through Maisemore, Hartpury, Corse
Staunton – near the Malverns now – then into a pub,
where I quaffed a foaming beaker of gingerbeer (price
2*d*) and turned off to Ryton, across roads puzzling on
the map, but asking questions of my own courteous
country men and women. Then as I neared
Redmarley (O the good county) I saw the sight which
had been my hope to see – Daffodils growing in the
orchards and lovely-green fields smiling at the sun.
Little knolls rising up continually on the unexpectant
eye, deep lanes (and still the uprooted disinherited
trees; not wasted to decay, I thought in consolation,
but nobly overthrown by a noble enemy: 'a Roman
valiantly conquered.'[15]) and a soil coloured of a
surpassing red, from which Redmarley gets its name.
That little village set under the shadow of the

---

[14] GA: G.41.24 and Hurd Transcript. It was probably written on 23
April.
[15] Gurney has substituted 'conquered' for 'vanquished' in this line
from *Anthony and Cleopatra*, IV. xiii.

Malverns and set with orchards thick and fair with
blossoms and flowers. Cowslips, daffodils, bluebells,
ladysmocks; all Shakespearian like the country – a
perfect setting for the old comedy.

Then a wandering thought became firm. Lascelles
Abercrombie and Wilfred Gibson both live at Ryton,
near my way. I would go see their houses. And when I
asked some pleasant smiling woman where Mr
Abercrombie lived, I was told 'The second house on
the left'. Then there came a dip of the road with a
gorgeous bit of redsandstone rock jutting out on the
road, then a double cottage with a sort of courtyard. I
stood hesitating for long with my eyes fixed on its
white front; made up my mind, went up and knocked.
Let it suffice to say that I spent 6 very full hours of joy
with Mrs Abercrombie, her husband is munition-
making in Liverpool, and acquired a rich memory. I
wheeled the pram, I did feats of daring to amuse the
three children, and talked books and music with Mrs
Abercrombie, the genius of the place; all set in blue of
the sky, green of the fields and leaves, and that red of
the soil. Abercrombie is very interested in music too,
and can read scores; his is a very wide versatile mind.

Then I left her with kind thoughts and words,
westward to Newent and Dymock, to take supper
finally at Minsterworth – but no laughter there
now. Mrs Harvey being a widow, and her three sons
in the army. But there was Bach for a while. Then
out to the night and Venus high in the air and black
vault studded with stars so fair as she but dear to me;
and most dear.

Here's a go! This is 9 oclock and the sergeant has
just stricken us dumb with the news of 'Night

operations 12.15 marching order.' 'Oh, the pain'! as our catchword runs. That gives you some notion of the way they work us now. I don't mind the hard work so much, but the cleaning!!!

I feel as if *Heldenleben*[16] were inadequate to express my feelings – pettily childish – O those buttons and buckles and boots! Hell to it, say I.

* * * *

22 May 1916 (KT)
(Written on a page torn from a small notebook)

My Dear Comtesse

Thank you for your letter, which shall be replied to when we get to France; and we leave tomorrow night or Wed morning. Here are the cushions. Please get me a valve for the green one and let me have it some time.

Yours affectionately
Ivor.

Love to everybody.

* * * *

---

[16] *Ein Heldenleben* ('A Hero's Life'), tone poem by Richard Strauss.

Among Gurney and Howells's close friends at the RCM were Arthur Benjamin, Arthur Bliss, and Francis Purcell Warren, a viola player. The nicknames of the five men began with 'B', a happy coincidence that in 1914 had prompted Howells to include portraits of all five in an orchestral suite, *The B's*, in which each movement represents one of the friends:

(i)	'Bublum'	–	Howells himself	(Overture)
(ii)	'Bartholomew'	–	Gurney	(Lament)
(iii)	'Blissy'	–	Bliss	(Scherzo)
(iv)	'Bunny'	–	Warren	(Mazurka)
(v)	'Benjee'	–	Benjamin	(March)

Apart from Marion Scott, other friends of Gurney's at the RCM included Sydney Shimmin, who became a music teacher and was, in 1946, the founder of the Cheltenham Bach Choir; and Ethel Voynich, a composer, translator and writer, whose best-known novel, *The Gadfly* (1897), was made into a film in 1955 for which Shostakovich famously provided the score.

Bliss, Warren, Benjamin and Shimmin all served in the First World War, a cause of ceaseless anxiety to the Director of the RCM, Sir Hubert Parry, who expressed his fear in a letter to Howells:

> Stanford sent me your letter about Gurney. I fully share in your anxieties. The thought of so many very gifted boys being in danger, such as Gurney and Fox and Benjamin and even Vaughan Williams, is always present with me. This is what horrible senseless war means – and we can do nothing. To put our views, that such beings are

capable of doing the world unique services, before the military authorities would surely appear to them absurd. I suppose there are thousands of others in other walks of life who are in the same case with us. Gurney's case I feel to be quite a special martyrdom. His mind is so full of thoughts and feeling far removed from crude barbarities that it seems almost monstrous. But war is monstrous and we have to take it as far as we can from the collective point of view. There is no consolation to be got out of that, but only something of the spirit which surprises those in the thick of it. I had a letter from Gurney yesterday full of Tolstoi and poetry and longings for the old beloved life, and a sight of the Cotswolds. It is cruel! He spoke of Easter leave. It's high time he had some [. . .].[17]

Bliss was wounded on the Somme, and Warren was killed at the Battle of Mons in 1917. Gurney corresponded with Howells, Shimmin and Ethel Voynich during the war, but the majority of his letters, by a very wide margin, were addressed to Marion Scott.[18]

Howells's health was never up to the standard required for service (he suffered from Graves' disease), and he was to remain in England throughout the war. On Saturday 12 February 1916, whilst waiting for his landlady to serve a meal, he took out a sheet of manuscript paper and wrote the opening bars of a Piano Quartet in A minor – it would prove to be his

[17] Christopher Palmer, *op cit*, p. 19.
[18] See R.K.R. Thornton, *Ivor Gurney: Collected Letters* (MidNAG Carcanet, 1991)

'most important chamber work to date, and is still regarded as one of the most significant works by a British composer of the period. He dedicated it to "The Hill at Chosen and Ivor Gurney who knows it" Although Howells did not give the work a programme as such, Marion Scott [. . .] was quite explicit in giving details of a 'nature' programme which helps colour the work's three movements'.[19]

When the first movement opens it is dawn, and the hill wind, pure, eternally free, and uplifting is blowing: gradually the greyness changes to crimson, the half-light to full radiance, mystery to vision, dawn to day.

The second movement is the hill upon a day in midsummer, and the thoughts are those which come as a man lies on the grass on his back gazing upward into the vast vault of the sky, seeing 'the giant clouds go royally', watching the blue depths of height untold flow outward to surrounding immensity until, floating on the flood of wonder, mind and soul are almost loosed from the earthly anchorage.

The finale is the hill in the month of March, with splendid winds of Spring rioting over it, and flashing in the exuberant rush, wild daffodils goldenly dancing (Ivor Gurney says there are no daffodils nearer Chosen than Dymock, but I leave the two Gloucesterians to settle this botanical detail). That is as much of the basis of the quartet as Herbert Howells yet allows to be told.[20]

---

[19] Paul Spicer, *Herbert Howells* (Seren, 1998), p. 46.
[20] Marion Scott, *The Music Student*, November 1918.

On 24th May 1916, Gurney sent Howells a postcard from Park House Camp:

Dear Howler

Finis est, or rather, Inceptus est (?). We go tomorrow. Little Howler, continue in thy path of life, blessing others and being blest, creating music and joy, never ceasing from the attempt to make English music what it should be, and calmly scornful-heedless of the critics. Go on and prosper, and Au revoir.

I.B.G.[21]

2

FRANCE AND BELGIUM

May 1916–September 1917

*The 2nd/5th Gloster Battalion sailed to
Le Havre aboard a troopship on 25th May 1916
and marched towards Flanders. Following
the long march they rested in the village of
Le Sart, a few miles north of Bethune, before
going into the trenches at Riez Bailleul for a week
of instruction under the London Welsh Regiment.
They returned to Le Sart on 8th June and, two
days later, moved into a reserve position at
Laventie. On 15th June they moved into the
front line in the Fauquissart – Laventie Sector
where they remained until 27th October 1916
when they marched south to join the carnage of
the Somme Offensive.*

FIELD SERVICE
POST CARD

To: Mrs Chapman,
St Michael's etc.

After deletions, printed
message reads:

   I am quite well
   I have received your
letter dated . . .
   Letter follows at first
opportunity
(Signed) I B Gurney
(date) 13/6/16

First Time In

After the dread tales and red yarns of the Line
Anything might have come to us; but the divine
Afterglow brought us up to a Welsh colony
Hiding in sandbag ditches, whispering consolatory
Soft foreign things. Then we were taken in
To low huts candle-lit, shaded close by slitten
Oilsheets, and there but boys gave us kind welcome,
So that we looked out as from the edge of home,
Sang us Welsh things, and changed all former notions
To human hopeful things. And the next day's guns
Nor any line-pangs ever quite could blot out
That strangely beautiful entry to war's rout;
Candles they gave us, precious and shared over-rations –
Ulysses found little more in his wanderings without doubt.
'David of the White Rock', the 'Slumber Song' so soft,
                                            and that
Beautiful tune to which roguish words by Welsh pit boys
Are sung — but never more beautiful than here under
                        The guns' noise.

Stars in a Dark Night

7 June 1916 (KT)

My Dear Chapmen

Whom I greet with best wishes, most particularly Arthur and the Governor who are soon to attain the seldom honour of a birthday. Well, we were not out long before we had been put a company at a time into the trenches. At least two companies, with two other regiments. And we had a strafe too, which caused a few casualties but not to me.

It is charged against me that I did not open a certain letter. As a matter of fact, the cushion was never undone. When I received it I decided that it was too good to use, and better to wait till the other valve arrived, which of course I sent for late. Please do not think I do not read *all* letters, even sentimental and religious. Could you but see the rush for letters here, and the disappointment on the faces of the unsuccessful, you would feel pleased indeed. I would send you souvenirs, shrapnel and such like – but that's all forbidden now.

The news of a present of a watch is good. It will save me languishing in gaol perhaps for being late. The chap I depend on for my horology is nearly as uncertain as myself, and I was thinking of dismissing him soon. It would amuse you to see me trying to talk French, but at any rate I can get what I want without much trouble.

My dear people, all of you, the remembrance of that last stay with you is refreshing to one who sleeps in barns, but there are some consolations. The faces and comradeship of the Welsh Regiment we are now with were worth going far to meet, and they sing their old songs. Picture my joy.

I regret to say that the Army sees to it that one has enough money on leave by dishing out only 5 francs a week to us, and that irregularly. We get also but a quarter loaf of bread, but the French bread is excellent – in great round slabs. Very grateful after the drier Army bread is its dampness and yielding quality. The chocolate is excellent, and the people very kind. It is surprising to see everything as usual very well within reach of the guns. They used to shell the villages but do not seem to now.

There is quite a fine church a few yards from me shattered but still noble, and under the shadow of it the estaminets are doing good trade – maybe with windows shattered, the children play; and the country a mile or so behind the firing line is green and peaceful as our Dear England's.

À Bon sante of all, but more especially of Messieurs Arthur and Le Pere.

Yours affectionately
Ivor

P.S. For goodness sake do not wait till you get my address – this would not be till 'aprés le guerre'; may be a long time yet. And you will be pleased to hear that we get letters pretty regularly, in or out of the trenches.

*   *   *   *

Gurney was always to spare the Chapmans descriptions of the worst horrors of war, but when he received a letter from Catherine Abercrombie, along with a copy of her husband's play, *Deborah*, he allowed himself, in his reply,[1] to reveal the impact of death's presence, perhaps because he knew that Lascelles Abercrombie was employed on war work at a munitions factory in Liverpool, far away from harm.

[. . .] Well we landed at one of the noblest – what do I say, the noblest town it has been my good fortune to see; I hope to speak to you of it some day. But we had not long to stay there or anywhere till we were marched here and put in trenches with another battalion for instruction. They were Welsh, mostly, and personally I feared a rather rough type. But, oh the joy, I crawled into a dugout, not high but fairly large, lit by a candle, and so met four of the most delightful young men that could be met anywhere. Thin faced and bright eyed, their faces showed beautifully against the soft glow of the candlelight, and their musical voices delightful after the long march at attention in silence. There was no sleep for me that night, I made up next day a little, but what then? We talked of Welsh folksong, of George Borrow, of Burns, of the R.C.M.; of – yes – of Oscar Wilde, Omar Khayyam, Shakespeare, and of the war; distant from us by 300 yards. Snipers were continually firing, and rockets – fairy lights they call them fired from a pistol – lit up the night outside.

[1] Hurd transcripts.

Every now and again a distant rumble of guns to remind us of the reason we were foregathered. They spoke of their friends dead or maimed in the bombardment, a bad one, of the night before, and in the face of their grief I sat there and for once self-forgetful, more or less, gave them all my love, for their tenderness, their steadfastness and kindness to raw fighters and *very* raw signallers. Well, we had two days like that, and played Auction Bridge, talked, read, smoked, and went through a trench-mortar strafe together.

Once we were standing outside our dugout cleaning mess tins, when a cuckoo sounded its call from the shattered wood at the back. What could I think of but Framilode, Minsterworth, Cranham, and the old haunts of home.

This Welshman turned to me passionately. 'Listen to that damned bird', he said. 'All through that bombardment in the pauses I could hear that infernal silly "Cuckoo, Cuckoo" sounding while Owen was lying in my arms covered with blood. How shall I ever listen again . . . !' He broke off, and I became aware of shame at the unholy joy that filled my artist's mind. And what a fine thin keen face he had, and what a voice – for speaking I mean. Gibson may have had this same thought as he listened to the cuckoo this spring. Shakespeare also maybe –

> O word of fear
> Unpleasing to a soldier's ear ...

* * * *

June 1916 (KT)

My Dear Old Winnie

Thank you for your jolly letter which I enjoyed very much, with all its bits of news and gossip. Bon. And I am glad to hear about Kitty's great success in her new sphere of existence.[2]

And, from my influential friend the Comtesse de Tilda how Arthur is getting on at le cricket. Bless his little heart. Stap me, but tis a sprightly youth. Also, it pleases me that you are so much in request as a vocalist. My dear kid, continue you in the straight and narrow way, take as pattern the high example set you by my good friends the Rushby-Smith girls and it will give me the greatest pleasure, apres le guerre to confer on you the famous order of the Icy Glare.

I suppose Ping-Pong is still impossible for you. Alas this is a horrible war. And they don't give us enough bread in it, confound 'em. He asked for bread and they gave him a stony look. Oliver Twist would have had a bad time out here I fear.

How is your frail body, too weak to bear all the strain as yet your spirit would put upon it? Anyway go on steadily: some day it will stand a lot. My jaws for instance have developed terrific crushing powers, absolutely unimaginable to the ordinary low down civilian.

Arthur and Micky shall have letters very soon, and but for the fact that another letter is overdue and these

---

[2] Kitty had joined the Land Army.

Micky

will go off tonight, they should have them now. Meanwhile, cheer up my estimable female, and hope for the end of the war which chiefly bores me. Though two nights ago it was sufficiently exciting. There is difficulty in showing where we are placed but opposite Lille will do maybe. Micky shall not have to wait long for a letter from Laventie as we are in reserve for a time. Good bye my chers enfants. Expect me to tea on Sunday.

Yours affectionately
Ivor

21 June 1916 (P)

My Dear Comtesse

You are as kind as ever, and your scones as good. It was delightful to get them, and they were eaten with great rejoicing in a little (signallers) barn at the back of a farm in Northern France – somewhere. But – may I say so? – While we are on reserve; in the villages, we can get everything almost we can afford. Tobacco is *much* cheaper than in England. The war taxes do not apply in Army canteens. Those cigarettes, which may have cost you 8*d*, would have cost 4*d* here. Soap and Cold Cream about the same price as with you. And then there is the enormous postage! We buy French bread – excellent stuff, and cakes. And chocolate is cheaper than the English. It is not nice to say so, but it is better to make presents of food in *money*. The more so as we get the benefit of the exchange.

This is bad to say, but everybody out here agrees. The more so as they pay us 5 francs only, instead of 10 as in England. Bread is all we are short of – the ASC steal it – and out of the trenches that is easy. *And we are not allowed to carry extra stuff outside haversacks* and in those there is no room.

Well, what of Russian news? All the puling pessimists and the toadies of Germany swept away by one fact – that the Russians got through in 9 hours at one place. This is great – glorious. We will no longer think by rule and measure a la Garvin, but according to our faith – freely and with courage.

The two souvenirs I send were picked up in a ruined bank next to a ruined convent here in this town – where we live in comparative peace so short a distance behind the firing line. I hope the kids will like them. Arthur and Winnie will make best use of them I think.

I am glad about Kitty, and believe the life will suit her. She has company and some definite interesting new work to do; and what colossal sum the 2/5 [2nd/5th Battalion] would give for that happy fate, God only knows. The motto of the British Army is 'Fed up, but carrying on'. Winnie must be proud she is so much in request. She is the kind of lady who will some day make herself useful if not indispensable in all sorts of ways.

Micky is at present une chere petite diable (feminine in this case) and unforgettable in any case. By the way I have already written you a letter. I hope you got it? I know that one letter has reached its destination HEAVILY CENSORED, so that the official eye is On Me.

The Katharine Tynan verses are perfectly charming in that War Poetry cutting. Sweet, original and truly felt. The rest – n'importe. I did not read the slip on Women's influence on Men. Il est vieux jeu. Arthur is making scores of C.B. Fry size now I hope. He will make a god bat, but don't let him tear himself to pieces as a bowler, and share time in the slips as a fielder. *Don't* forget. The news about Mr Rushby Smith is astonishing but I bear up.[3] Go and do thou likewise.

Now I go for half an hour to a café where French may be painfully learnt at the cost of two cups – charming people.

Good bye everybody

Many happy returns and may I be there to share the next.

Yours affection.
Ivor

Congrats to the Gov: and Arthur

3 The Revd Rushby-Smith was appointed Canon of Oxford.

Laventie

One would remember still
Meadows and low hill
Laventie was, as to the Line and elm row
Growing through green strength wounded, as home elms grow.
Shimmer of Summer there and blue Autumn mists
Seen from trench-ditch winding in mazy twists.
The Australian gunners in close flowery hiding
Cunning found out at last, and smashed in the unspeakable lists.
And the guns in the smashed wood thumping and grinding.

The letters written there, and received there,
Books, cakes, cigarettes in a parish of famine,
And leaks in rainy times with general all-damning.
The crater, and carrying of gas cylinders on two sticks
(Pain past comparison and far past right agony gone)
Strained hopelessly of heart and frame at first fix.

Café-au-lait in dugouts on Tommies' cookers,
Cursed minnie-werfs, thirst in eighteen-hour summer.
The Australian miners clayed, and the being afraid
Before strafes, sultry August dusk time than Death dumber –
And the cooler hush after the strafe, and the long night wait –
The relief of first dawn, the crawling out to look at it,
Wonder divine of Dawn, man hesitating before Heaven's gate.
Lovely aerial beetles of wonderful scintillate
Strangest interest, and puffs of soft purest white –
Soaking light, dispersing colouring for fancy's delight.

Of Maconachie, Paxton, Tickler, and Gloucester's Stephens;
Fray Bentos, Spiller and Baker, odds and evens
Of trench food, but the everlasting clean craving
For bread, the pure thing, blessèd beyond saving.
Canteen disappointments, and the keen boy braving
Bullets or such for grouse roused surprisingly through
(Halfway) Stand-to.
And the shell nearly blunted my razor at shaving;
Tilleloy, Fauquissart, Neuve chapelle, and mud like glue.

But Laventie, most of all, I think is to soldiers
The town itself with plane trees, and small-spa air;
And vin, rouge-blanc, chocolat, citron, grenadine:
One might buy in small delectable cafés there.
The broken church, and vegetable fields bare;
Neat French market town look so clean,
And the charity, amiability of North French air.

Like water flowing beneath the dark plough and high Heaven,
Music's delight to please the poet pack-marching there.

S TARS IN A D ARK N IGHT

22 June 1916 (G)

My Dear Comtesse

No present could have given me more pleasure than this one. The very best, and 'twill no doubt save me much trouble. We have just come out of trenches after a strafe that a man who had been through Loos described as being worse than Loos while it lasted. Well, it is as well to do the thing properly. I am glad to be out of it, glad to have been through it, and the Glosters are a good crowd, bless 'em. But it seems doubtful whether I should ever see High Wycombe again. I think 6 inches or so lower would have given much opportunity for damage to 10 high explosives, which burst about 30 yards behind us. I had my eye, or part of it round the corner of the bay, and it was a fine sight. Also I was as cool as now, writing this letter. This suits me, but it don't put my belly right, or make me less introspective, confound it! All I wished for was to play the G minor Prelude from Part II – Bach,[4] when it was all over. But there was only those brick biscuits to chew. I hope me generous benefactress you are pretty well and kicking fairly strongly. I hope for a nice blighty to come and see you all before long.

> *Yours affectionately*
> Ivor Gurney

---

[4] J.S. Bach, *Das Wohltemperierte Klavier II* (*The Well-/Tempered Clavier, Book II*), Prelude XVI, in G minor.

The church at Laventie, 1916

Arthur

STARS IN A DARK NIGHT

22 June 1916 (G)

My Dear Arthur

Go you on and prosper, and rise from the 'not out 0' to the 'not out 20'. Then from 'not out 0' 1st eleven to undreamed of heights. It only means coolness with you, who have all the other gifts, necessary for big scores. You should have bits of shrapnel and so on, if it were allowed to send them, but the official foot is hard down on such little presents. Lying in my dugout or funkhole the other day, I became too bored to read serious stuff, or write letters: so turning my attention to the few filthy magazines strewn around, left by the last visitants, I became aware of a thrilling boys tale of 3 scouts who apparently played the very deuce and all with the Germans. It was so absolutely unlike the real thing that I read quite a lot of it, and laughed a great deal. At present it is chiefly – sticking it; with the prospect of a big bust soon. Machine guns all going at once are the terrifying things, and I don't like 'em.

Everything goes well with you I hope. You've got brains enough to do the lessons they will give you, if you take it coolly and don't worry. The only way I can clean equipment and rifle (and O how I hate doing that silly old job over and over again) is to do the first thing – any 'first thing', and let the rest sort itself out.

Here is a song our men sang when the last strafe was at its hottest – a very popular song about here; but not military.

I want to go home, I want to go home
The whizzbangs and shrapnel they whistle and roar.
I don't want to go in the trenches no more,
Take me over the sea,
Where the Alleman can't catch me.
O my! I don't want to die.
I *want* to go home.

Not a brave song, but brave men sing it.

Yours affectionately
Ivor

29 June 1916 (KT)

My Dear Mr C.

Nothing, as your acute intellect will perceive, has yet happened to me. I am still in one piece, but a bored, humiliated, altogether fed up piece of humanity, who looks for the end of the war to deliver him from bondage. And just as I reach this, it turns out that a German aeroplane is soaring over us, and so our anti-aircraft guns are potting and sending lovely little white fleeces of cloud high up against a quite perfect blue. But Fritz when he attempts these daring feats takes good care to fly as near Heaven as he will ever get, whereas our men fly low and saunter along – a cheering sight.

When you write, as I hope you will, please send me some facts about munitions. As how a piece of waste land, chiefly distinguished for its fine vein of sardine and pineapple tins, has now been turned into the most amazing group of works turning out by thousands of tons a day shells of the most remarkable destructivity. Any little facts like this, or the Rev Horatio Bottomley's[5] prediction of the close of hostilities in June before last; anything like this will bring a smile to the wasted lips of a soldier. But don't breathe a word of anything nasty happening after the end of August or else you will run the risk of extreme unpopularity with the gallant defenders of your country.

I hear that you are frightfully busy and so out of mischief. What would I not give for the chance of good clean honest work, instead of the aimless mucking-about! I envy Kitty with all my heart, so do all we. She seems to have done very well, and to be 'busy, well and jolly . . . ' Oh squirms from the Gallery! Almost two years ago I was driving a tedding machine with the Severn, May Hill, Malverns and Cotswold to look at. But all these joys have descended upon the women, who seem quite capable of doing the job. I wish they would tackle this one. No 3895 is always ready to resign.[6]

With best wishes

Yours affectionately
Ivor Gurney

---

[5] Horatio Bottomley, a discredited bankrupt before the war, became 'the People's Tribune' and was the most successful of recruiting orators, pulling in many recruits; he also made a fortune from admission charges, money that he squandered on horse-racing, women and champagne.

[6] Gurney's first Army number.

The trenches at Laventie

27 July 1916 (P)

My Dear Count

(that is if you *do* count) I snatch a peaceful hour at 1 a.m. to assure you that those cigars were far better than anything I could have made from your parcel-wrappings. Indeed, I will go so far as to say that they tasted as if they had been really bought at a shop, had it not been war-time, and if homemade, do (or did) you great credit. They tell me you have taken up Bowls, which seems to show that you recognise your status and disabilities at last, and will soon be content to yield up the reins into your son's hands – a promising youth of considerable military reputation.

You have not submitted any further names of offers of appointments to my judgement, so suppose that there are no further offers. Or is it that there are too many?

Well, well, I will not condemn unheard.

Things are moving out here as you may have heard lately. Do you happen to know whether our Nobs consider the thing satisfactory?[7] I thought you may have gathered some notion. War don't suit me, sir, and I don't care who knows it, unless the Kaiser gets trying any of his tricks. And to hide in holes from flying whizzbangs and gradually to approach the state of doddering grandmotherliness is not my idea of Fun. But here's the job ready to my hand, and what must be done, shall be done. Though selling chip potatoes in

---

[7] The Somme offensive began on 1 July 1916. There were 60,000 British casualties on the first day of the battle, 20,000 of them dead.

Hell seems to us occasionally to have merits superior to this life.

Well, someday I may return to a life with kids in it, and flowers and a real white tablecloth, and more cigars.

Meanwhile Cheero, my giddy Goods Manager.

Yours affectionately
Ivor

27 July 1916 (P)

My Dear Comtesse

(Whack! there goes another mosquito!)

It was delightful to get your letter tonight, and to renew my acquaintance with pleasant memories.

I am glad that Kitty seems to have dropped into her proper place, and in a nice direction too. Syde is quite unknown to me, however. Daddy I hope is as expert at bowls as at Chess, though if he has been boasting, I withdraw all that. He sent some good cigars though. It was all of a good parcel that. The oatcake was a Creation, an inspiration of high degree. The cake was good enough, and the tallow candles of a taste the most delectable. Cigars too, thought I. Buck ye up! thought I! Wha's the warl' comin' tae? (I believe that may pass). Luckily it got me in the trenches, and so there was no need either to carry it, or eat it hastily. Also, we have been out of civilisation so much that I am quite wealthy – for me.

In trenches one cannot buy, and then parcels are as manna of the best make.

What a pity it was you missed the songs. I knew myself very late, but thought the letter might just scrape home in time to give you notice. There nearly was a disaster about the singer, but not quite – thanks to H.N.H. and Miss Scott, who hung on like valiant limpets.[8]

But how can one concentrate one's mind on higher affairs when these beastly mosquito's are gradually biting one to a shadow? It's no possible wumman. But thank you for your letter. My intellects wanted something restful and homey, and your letter supplied the want. St Thomas a Kempis is a ruddy unmitigated bore. I am afraid High Wycombe will receive some bad news soon from this way. If you send me a book ever, let it be small. I ask no more, so low and humble have my desires become. Pity the poor egotist!

Love to everybody.

Yours affectionately
Ivor

August 1916 (KT)

My Dear Winnie

I did not write on your birthday.[9] Too many things cropped up for that. But it was remembered; the first

---

[8] Herbert Howells and Marion Scott had arranged for a performance of Gurney's *Five Elizabethan Songs* at the RCM.
[9] Winnie's sixteenth birthday was on 10th August.

since Arthur's that is set down in the book your revered Pa bestowed upon me. And now you are down at Perranporth, listening to the sea. Possibly bathing in it. 'Fore Jove, a lucky wench! No bathe for me this lovely morning but a dip in an old biscuit tin – such terrible hardships do war heroes undergo. But don't let this disturb you. Please enjoy yourself double for both our sakes. And let the others follow your excellent example. Let your sand castles outdo the windiest vapourings of Sir Walter Scott, and your mud-pies outdo those of the Ritz or Carlton.

And tell me how the rabbits get on, and if they are still cannibalistic in their nasty habits, which is distressing.

In my next letter, which will be to Micky, there will be found a collection of be-yutiful drawings or stupendous epics; I have not yet decided which. However it is for me much easier to say 'The Cow stands on four legs' than to depict the animal caught in the act. I can do the four legs with tolerable success. It is planting the cow on top of them that bothers me. The man who invented cows was a clever chap, and should be heartily congratulated by the Affiliated Society of Cunning Milkmen. Ping-pong is more na pooh than ever I suppose. But wouldn't a hard wet sand table look well with little celluloid balls dancing about it? I wish I were with you to experiment, and to run races on the sand or to take down Arthur's pride at le criquette.

Yours affectionately
Ivor

*　*　*　*

On 16th August 1916, Will Harvey's company also moved into position south of Laventie, and the next morning he and Gurney were able to meet briefly. Harvey, by now a Lieutenant, lent Gurney a copy of Robert Bridges's *The Spirit of Man*. Later in the day he set out alone to reconnoitre in No-Man's Land as a preparation for leading a patrol that night; he did not return.

Believing his best friend to be dead, Gurney wrote to Marion Scott:

[. . .] Willy Harvey, my best friend, went out on patrol a week ago, and never came back. It does not make very much difference; for two years I have had only the most fleeting glimpses of him, but we were firm enough in friendship, and I do not look ever for a closer bond, though I live long and am as lucky in friendship as heretofore.

He was full of unsatisfied longings. A Doctor would have called it neurasthenia, but that term covers many things, and in him it meant partly an idealism that could not be contented with realities. His ordinary look was gloomy, but on being spoken to he gladdened one with the most beautiful of smiles, the most considerate courtesy of manner. Being self-absorbed, he was nevertheless nobly unselfish at most times, and all who knew him and understood him, must not have liked him merely, but have loved him. Had he lived, a great poet might have developed from him, could he only obtain the gift of serenity . . . If the Fates send that I live to a great age and attain fulness of days and honour, nothing can alter my memory of him or the evenings we spent together at Minsterworth. My thoughts of Bach and all firelit frosty evenings will be full of him, and the perfectest evening of Autumn will but recall him the more vividly to my memory. He is my friend, and nothing can alter that, and if I have the good fortune ever to meet with such another, he has a golden memory to contend with. A thing not easy [. . .].[10]

'All who knew him and understood him, must not have liked him merely, but have loved him', and Gurney clearly loved Harvey in this sense. Sarah Anne Kane's love for Harvey was, of course, an altogether more fervent, intense emotion; but the belief that his dear friend was dead proved the catalyst in establishing Gurney as the master of a wholly individual and original poetic voice.

The resultant poem, 'To His Love', bore an earlier title, 'On a Dead Poet', but Gurney altered his first draft, transforming a predictable lament into a deeply personal and, at the same time, ambiguous masterpiece.

Inevitably, a poem that could well have been addressed to Harvey's fiancée, Sarah Anne, has also been interpreted as carrying an homoerotic charge. And it seems very possible that at the outset of their especially close friendship, Harvey and Gurney may have shared sensations of that pure 'love' not uncommon amongst adolescents of either sex – an interpretation thought likely by Harvey's daughter.[11] It

[10] GA: G.41.3.5. Harvey had actually been captured by the Germans, and spent the rest of the war in POW camps.
[11] Reminiscences of Eileen Griffiths (*née* Harvey).

Winnie and Kitty

would, however, be a mistake to apply a twenty-first century interpretation of 'love' to an emotion expressed in an earlier, less permissive time. Gurney and Harvey were 'firm in friendship', but when asked if Ivor Gurney might have been an homosexual, Herbert Howells repudiated any such suggestion with uncharacteristic anger: 'He would have died first!'[12]

[12] Reminiscences of Michael Hurd.

To His Love

He's gone, and all our plans
    Are useless indeed.
We'll walk no more on Cotswold
    Where the sheep feed
    Quietly and take no heed.

His body that was so quick
    Is not as you
Knew it, on Severn river
    Under the blue
    Driving our small boat through.

You would not know him now . . .
    But still he died
Nobly, so cover him over
    With violets of pride
    Purple from Severn side.

Cover him, cover him soon!
    And with thick-set
Masses of memoried flowers –
    Hide that red wet
    Thing I must somehow forget.

December 1916 (KT)

(Headed: Address in future only name, co, reg: and BEF France)

My Dear Old Winnie

Still a war on! and I still in it! How I envy Kitty, and her rise in wages! It is really an achievement though, to have stuck at hard work and got a rise. And I congratulate her very much. Cheero!

You must hurry up and get strong and fit and well: do stunts on the parallel bars, and lift dumbells by nervous convulsion only. On such meagre routine do the great thrive. Dear kid; it is a different sort of life now to the December of two years ago. Ping-pong between the lines has been stopped, and I no longer play accompaniments for the Germans. Soon they will stop us inviting each other to tea. The German spy system is excellent. Wonderful! They manage to find out when any oatcake arrives for me, and if I do not ask them over, invariably raid before they think it all gone. I will spend the last drop of my blood to defend the last crumb of La Comtesse's oatmeal.

I thought of you on All Hallows eve (Hallowmas Eve, isn't it?) and imagined you performing some strange Gaelic rites of memory and sanctification. I hope you had 'Sweet Polly Oliver' or the 'Bay of Biscay' in memory of one not yet needing rites but only remembrance.

The soap I am using now, but not the baccy. The oatcake had but a short life, but an appreciated one. Goodbye and love to everybody.

Your affectionate friend
Ivor

Stars in a Dark Night

December 1916 (KT)

My Dear Winnie

Here is a tiny note for you which may get to you by Xmas Day, or long before, or long after, as the case may be. Anyway enjoy it, my dear enemy (at ping-pong). Alas! I know not if the sport of ping-pong still flourishes anywhere in the land.

Lately, I have shirked much on account of a disturbed interior. RAMC, Rest Station, and now on a job – a comparatively nice one to do with water-carts. This is all very well, but I have had no letters. Please write to me. Private Gurney 2/5 Glos: attached Sanitary Section 61st Div HQ. That will reach me I think

I wonder how you have been lately with all this grey unpleasant weather. No bon! no bon!

And Arthur and Mick both of whom shall receive the polished epistle. Cheero!

There will be no long walk for us this Xmas – but there is a good chance of leave soon, and then who knows what wonders will happen? Yes, Leave. When? Don't know, but a good leave – no skimpy allowance of a day.

My dear kids there will be joy then and much galumphing, even though they be meatless days, and only 3 courses.

Does the new Vicar appreciate Mrs Chapman's excellent scones? I hope he has not taken my place – in the slippers only large enough because of the holes. Don't let him have any oatcakes. I have heard and met so many Scots lately on this job, that I have tasted oatcake quite often in fancy lately.

O to do so in reality.

Bon O Bon

Yours affect: Ivor

New Year 1917 (KT)

My Dear Old Win

Still here and not there, as is perhaps to be expected. No leave yet, that is to say; but who knows? I may arrive home from the office tonight and find a telegram 'Will you come and teach me how? Lloyd George' (reply half-prepaid). Or 'Do stop them, old man – Wilhelm' (not prepaid) lying on the hall table. This might mean quite a few days in Blighty, in which case I shall hurry at once to St Micks (Collis castelli – Castle Hill) and present my never-for-one-single-phsycological [*sic*]-moment-to-be-forgotten Winifred with the one souvenir I have – the tattered remains of a G. pocket book – if it lasts till then.

I hope Christmas went off all right and fine – that Daddy was not grumpy and La Comtesse grumpy at his grumpiness. I trust you danced the roundelay and Fa-la-la-ed to any extent. Stap me, had I been there, would not I have taken part in those innocent revels? Yea, by the to [*sic*] old Pig of Brixham, marry, so would I!

And how's Arthur and how's that little imp of restlessness Micky, the human Soap-Bubble? How many goals has Arthur the Hope of his Side managed to score?

I want to know all Mrs. It is port wine oatcakes and chews of bacca to me. Hogmanay was happy and rowdy just round here – happier than it was in Scotland the men come back from leave say.

Well I hope High Wycombe put some go into the parting kick.

Good bye

Yours affectionately
Ivor

In February 1917 Gurney's battalion moved to the Ablaincourt Sector and followed the German strategic withdrawal eastward from village to village. At Caulaincourt two companies of the Glosters, including Gurney's, sheltered in a mausoleum in the graveyard, the only building still standing in the village. On 31st March the battalion reached Vermand. On Good Friday night Gurney was wounded in the arm, necessitating his hospitalisation in Rouen, where he remained for six weeks.

At the end of May 1917 Gurney, a crack shot, was transferred to a machine-gun company and given a new Service number (241281), remaining with the 2nd/5th Glosters, who were now at the Arras front.

POSTCARD addressed to:
Winnie, St Michael's, etc.
View of Rouen.

No message.

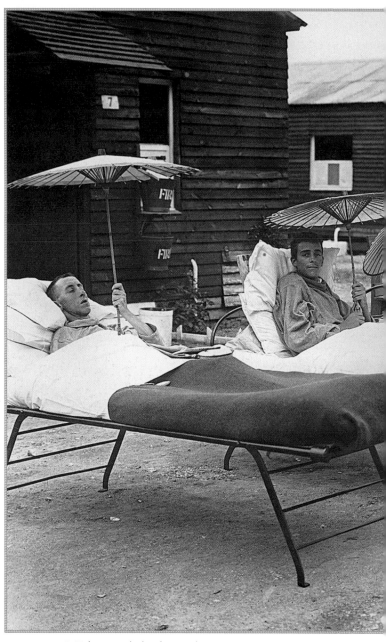

British wounded in hospital, Rouen, 1 June 1917

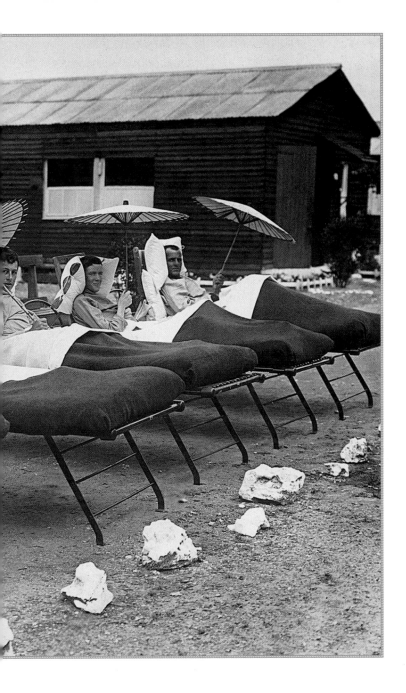

13 May 1917 (KT)

My Dear Winnie

I hope you have received the cards I sent a few days ago, and like them. Also that you poor creatures are not absolutely starving in poor old Blighty. They will soon prohibit the sending of cakes out here, and about time if all tales are true; you must be a nest of walking skeletons.

Are you all pretty well now? The weather is certainly not cold, anyway, and you can get out. Do you play games ever? How is the Comtesse, worker of miracles

Kitty (on right) with two Land Army friends, 1916

out of oatmeal and plain flour? and Daddy with his weight of natural cares? How is Arthur doing at Cricket? As for Mick, I never could believe her sick till the mourning cards were issued, and she is probably as naughty (and nice) as ever.

They are chucking us out at any time now – Hup the line: Hover the top and the best of luck. Tuesday must see us off I think, so please write to the Batt: in future. The next wound I have will bring me more luck, or else I shall have cutting remarks to make to the Lord Almighty. How are the Christ Church people – his special delegates and assistants. And how is the Pet Lootenant[13] doing in France?

I have lost your mascot that you put in my overcoat. It had stayed there carefully cherished until Good Friday Night when we went over, and since then – well I shall be lucky if I see ever a thing again.

What must the High Wycombe hills look like now! Great clouds of miraculous green, green that looks alive and gifted with a voice.

Here endeth the last letter from the Base.

Yours affectionately
Ivor

---

13 Lieutenant Wildsmyth, a family friend of the Chapmans.

The trenches at Laventie

An old gun position in Sanctuary Wood, in the Ypres sector,
25 October 1917

Remains of a line of German strong points near St Julien,
12 October 1917

The Target

I shot him, and it had to be
One of us! 'Twas him or me.
'Couldn't be helped,' and none can blame
Me, for you would do the same.

My mother, she can't sleep for fear
Of what might be a-happening here
To me. Perhaps it might be best
To die, and set her fears at rest.

For worst is worst, and worry's done.
Perhaps he was the only son ...
Yet God keeps still, and does not say
A word of guidance any way.

Well, if they get me, first I'll find
That boy, and tell him all my mind,
And see who felt the bullet worst,
And ask his pardon, if I durst.

All's a tangle. Here's my job,
A man might rave, or shout, or sob;
And God He takes no sort of heed.
This is a bloody mess indeed.

3
BLIGHTY

In August 1917, the Glosters moved north to the Ypres front. By early September they were in St Julien facing the Passchendaele Ridge. Ivor Gurney was gassed.

In September 1917 Gurney was evacuated from France to the Bangour War Hospital, near Edinburgh. Whilst there he met and fell in love with one of his nurses, Annie Nelson Drummond, and seems to have had reason to believe that his feelings were reciprocated. She was to become his 'Hawthornden' (a literary pun on 'Drummond', *i.e.* 'Drummond of Hawthornden', the poet William Drummond, 1585–1649) and the dedicatee of songs and verse. Gurney wrote excitedly about her in a letter to Howells:

[. . .] Annie Nelson Drummond is older than I thought – born sooner I mean. She is 30 years old and most perfectly enchanting. She has a pretty figure, pretty hair, fine eyes, pretty hands and arms *and* walk. A charming voice, pretty ears, a resolute little mouth. With a great love in her she is glad to give when the time comes. In Hospital, the first thing that would strike you is 'her guarded flame'. There was a mask on her face more impenetrable than on any other woman I have ever seen. (But that has gone for me). In fact (at a guess) I think it will disappear now she has found someone whom she thinks worthy.

A not unimportant fact was revealed by one of the patients at hospital – a fine chap – I believe she has money. Just think of it! Pure good luck, if it is true (as I believe it is). But she is more charming and tender and deep than you will believe till you see her.

O Erbert, O Erbert . . .
I forgot my body walking with her; a thing that hasn't happened
since..................... when?
I really don't know [. . .].[1]

Professionally, too, Gurney was beginning to make his mark in 1917. Herbert Howells transcribed for orchestra two of Gurney's songs, *In Flanders* and *By a Bierside*, both of which were performed under Stanford's direction at RCM concerts in 1917 and 1919; and in October 1917, Sidgwick & Jackson published *Severn and Somme*, a collection of forty-six of Gurney's poems. However, he was not content, finding it difficult to adjust to the quiet hospital life. He considered himself a 'wangler' but dreaded a return to the trenches, which full recovery threatened.

By early November he was fit enough to leave hospital but, in a letter to Marion Scott, wrote that 'There's a bit of luck; owing to slight indigestion ('presumably due to gas; wink, wink!'), I am to go to Command Depot for two months – a sort of Con[valescent] Camp in Khaki.[2] He was not to be sent back straight away. Instead, after a few days' leave spent with the Chapmans in High Wycombe and at home in Gloucester, he was posted to a signalling course at the Command Depot, Seaton Delaval, Northumberland.

After Gurney left Bangour, he and Miss Drummond continued to correspond, and his hopes of a happy

[1] GA: G.3.32.
[2] GA: G.41.152a.

future with her continued to grow, but he found the camp at Seaton Delaval a 'freezing, ugly, uncomfortable Hell of a Hole'.[3] Life there was cold and meaningless to him; there was no comradeship comparable with that which, in adversity, he had enjoyed in France, and which had inspired him then, and very soon his old enemy 'neurasthenia' began to haunt him once more, as it had before 1914.

In February 1918 he was returned to hospital in Newcastle-upon-Tyne, and from there to Brancepeth Castle, Durham, for convalescence and training. For a while his symptoms seem to have subsided, and on 12th March he wrote to Howells from Brancepeth: 'I am happy today with a letter from A.N.D. after another, both charming, so shake hands; and her presence is strong on me as I write'.[4] Once again, he was able to compose – then, in late March, in a letter to Marion Scott, he revealed that:

> Yesterday I felt and talked to (I am serious) the spirit of Beethoven.
>
> No, there is no exclamation mark behind that, because such a statement is past ordinary ways of expressing surprise. But you know how sceptical I was of any such thing before.
>
> It means I have reached higher than ever before – in spite of the dirt and coarseness and selfishness of so much of me. Something happened the day before which considerably lessened this and lightened my

[3] GA: G.41.163.
[4] GA: G.3.23.

gloom. What it was I shall not tell you, but it was the strangest and most terrible spiritual adventure [. . .].[5]

Marion Scott's father had been an active member of the Society for Psychical Research since 1884; Arthur Conan Doyle was also a member, and a welcome guest at the Scott household.[6] Marion Scott would almost certainly have discussed her father's metaphysical philosophy with Gurney, and he may have felt no qualms in telling her about his encounter with 'Old Ludwig'. Even so, although he felt a spiritual uplifting through this experience, he knew that a more sinister interpretation could be put upon it. He ends: 'This letter is quite sane, n'est ce pas?'

By May, his mental condition had worsened. He was sent to Lord Derby's War Hospital, Warrington, but, in spite of his pre-war history of 'neurasthenia', itself a coverall diagnosis, Gurney's illness was described vaguely as a 'nervous breakdown from deferred shell-shock'.

At about this time Annie Drummond severed her correspondence with Gurney, a devastating blow that could not have come at a worse moment; his mind descended into black despair. On 19th June he wrote goodbye letters to Marion Scott, Sir Hubert Parry and Sir Charles Stanford: 'I know that you would rather know me dead than mad'. Intending suicide he wandered off to the canal – but courage to end his life failed him. Comradeship, love and hope – all seemed to have deserted him. He was escorted back to hospital,

[5] GA: G.70.6
[6] See Pamela Blevins, 'Marion Scott and Conan Doyle', *Ivor Gurney Society Newsletter*, No. 33, September 2003.

pleading with the doctors to send him to an asylum. Marion Scott and John Haines visited him separately, and on 1st July Haines wrote to Miss Scott:

[. . .] I heard from Ivor this morning – a postcard, and have written to him again. I enclose two letters received by me today from Abercrombie: they speak for themselves. I hope Canon Stevens will look him up soon. Warrington is the most detestable place I have ever spent six hours in, without exception, and the place would drive me mad, despite my lack of genius, in a very few weeks. How Gurney must dislike it I can well imagine. On the other hand I don't recommend the idea of any mental place very near Gloucester (they abound), nor do I think he should be allowed to go to his people until he is better than he is now: the father is too delicate and the mother too nervy.[7]

In fact, Ivor's father was suffering from terminal cancer. On 4th July, Ivor was transferred to the Middlesex War Hospital at Napsbury, St Albans, and there he remained until his discharge from the Army in October 1918 with a pension of twelve shillings per week.

The war ended in November.

*   *   *   *

[7] Michael Hurd, *op cit*, p. 125.

1 November 1917 (KT)   B2
                                                   The Camp
                                                    Bangour
                                             Near Edinburgh

My Dear Winnie

Here's t'ye, my bonnie lass, and don't you forget it. Soon the fatal chuckout will come and before going out I be granted a golden holiday from the Army. On which happy occasion you are to behold me once again, a gallant sojer with a loathing of everything in the whole bangshoot except the men chiefly oppressed.

Fair and charming damsel, once again will I present my respects to you, and tell you All about Myself, and walk up Keep Hill, and read and douse the glim late, and stick my feet on the mantlepiece in disreputable old slippers, and smoke a guggly churchwarden, and bless you my child, and wish I was a fixture for a while, and tootle the freudlich Bach and the triste Chopin, and frowst, and behave myself as though I were in a properly-conducted family of high ethical status.

I wonder whether I shall do all this? Je ne sais pas; anyway I will cherish the Chapman family in my bosom and criticise Haig's strategy as though I knew all about it.

Yours affectionately
Ivor

O yes, and you can say something every now and then.

17 November 1917 (KT)

My Dear Winnie

Here is a book I thought you would like; I hope you won't mind the markings: they are simply what pleased me. Dear old kid it was nice to see you, and nicer to see you again. At present, or at least on Monday I am to be put on a signalling course to last from 2 to 4 months; time to think of a commission after that, old girl.

The copies of my book[8] have not yet come, and I can't afford to buy any more. Directly it comes you shall have one. The papers have been kind to it – especially *The Times* and *Morning Post*. Did you take away the photo of yourself from the set I had? If so, you lay yourself open to extreme penalties, and utmost rigour of the law.

This place is a pit village, ugly enough but the (rather tame) sea is only 4 miles away, and the wind roars continually. This is the address.

Pte Gurney 241281
C Coy, 4th Reserve Batt:
Gloucesters
Seaton Delaval
Northumberland

Has Kitty got a new post yet? I hope she will get as good a one as she deserves. I hope everybody is well,

---

[8] *Severn and Somme.*

Mammy, Daddy and the brats Arthur and Micky, who has such a persuasive tongue.

Goodbye best wishes to you and everybody

Yours affectionately
Ivor

[Written at head of letter] Paper and String not to hand. Book comes when they come.

Companion–North-East Dugout

He talked of Africa,
   That fat and easy man.
I'd but to say a word,
   And straight the tales began.

And when I'd wish to read,
   That man would not disclose
A thought of harm, but sleep;
   Hard-breathing through his nose.

Then when I'd wish to hear
   More tales of Africa,
'Twas but to wake him up,
   And but a word to say

To press a button, and
   Keep quiet; nothing more;
For tales of stretching veldt,
   Kaffir and sullen Boer.

O what a lovely friend!
   O quiet easy life!
I wonder if his sister
   Would care to be my wife . . . .

[One of six *Hospital Pictures*, dedicated to 'The Nurses of Ward 24, Bangour War Hospital, near Edinburgh].

November 1917 (KT)   Pte Gurney 241281
                                       C Coy 4th Res: Batt:
                                           Gloucesters

My Dear Winnie

That blooming book has got stolen, I suppose, for no memory of sending it to you do I remember.

It was, poor thing, *The Old Country*, a YMCA book, which had some good stuff. Still, here's one of the most lovely little books I know.[9]

'The Old Bed' is simply perfect.

The first five Sonnets very good.

'I saw three pigs a riding', 'Tenants' and some more first rate. This is very precious to me, Wilfred Gibson is a master.

Sorry you haven't had my book yet. S and Js are slow.

The Times, *Morning Post* and *Telegraph* have liked it. With love to you all.

Yours affectionately
Ivor Gurney

Where's that photograph? What! What!

---

[9] Wilfrid Gibson, *Friends*.

Turmut Hoeing

I straightened my back from turmut hoeing
    And saw, with suddenly opened eyes,
Tall trees, a meadow ripe for mowing,
    And azure June's cloud-circled skies.

Below, the earth was beautiful
    Of touch and colour, fair each weed,
But Heaven's high beauty held me still,
    Only of music had I need.

And the white-clad girl at the old farm,
    Who smiled and looked across at me,
Dumb was held by that strong charm
    Of cloud-ships sailing a foamless sea.

[Written at the Middlesex War Hospital, Napsbury].

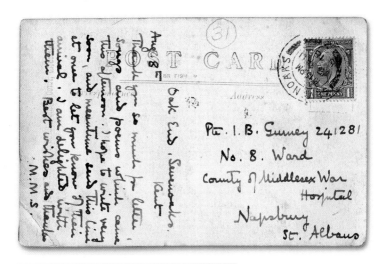

POSTCARD
From: Marion Scott
To: Pte I.B. Gurney
241281, No. 8 Ward
County of Middlesex
War Hospital etc.

August 8th,

Thankyou so much for
letter, songs and poems
which came this
afternoon. I hope to
write very soon, and
meantime send this line
at once to let you know
of their arrival. I am
delighted with them.
Best wishes and thanks
(Signed) M.M.S.

August 1918 (KT)

No 8 Ward
Middlesex War Hospital
Napsbury

My Dear Winnie

There's 10 minutes or so to pass before breakfast, and you shall have the benefit thereof. The Most Gracious Comtesse has received a letter from me lately I believe (my head's like a colander, and cannot hold much) but if this is not so she shall receive fullest consideration or notification of the same.

I wonder whether you are more stately than once you were, and what new accomplishments have come to you in the past year – whether you can make Simnel Cakes or burnish halberds or starch ruffs; or pickle peppercorns or any of a hundred useful things to be known by the young of that species, woman.

My certes there's a whole world of accomplishments that has come to me here. Polishing floors, rubbing brasses, washing pots, pans, kettles, floors: hoeing mangels and turmuts! ('Give I the turmut hoeing'). You see this is a new list – in which piano playing does not appear – for though the spirit is willing, the flesh is weak enough to quail before the looks of some folk here when they look up from cards or snoozing with a look either of amazed contempt or bitter anger! Well, well, there is always something to put up with in this crocky old world of tears. But of this I hope there is no trace at Perran. Don't get 'flu' or any other silly old disease. What do you do with your time – is it cricket, sand castles or mud pies? Would that this poor mortal were with you dashing about, and finding out the colour of sea water from the depth of a yard.

Comme ça, m'selle! Observe the dash from a height –
the slow float and the gradual return!! A masterpiece,
without doubt. I hope soon to be in a position to do such
mad delightful things, and then great works without
number (Symphony No 8 dedicated to Winifred
Chapman) will simply leak from my pen. Arthur shall
have a special portrait in music, of him making a
century at full speed with beaucoup boundaries. Until
then, ma chère mamselle I suscribe [*sic*] myself, with love

Yours affectionately
Ivor

Writing to Marion Scott on 11th September 1918,[10] Gurney enclosed a draft of his poem 'The Poplar', which was to be published in *War's Embers*, dedicated to Micky Chapman.

The Poplar

A tall slim poplar
   That dances in
A hidden corner
   Of the old garden,
What is it in you
   Makes communion
With this wind of Autumn
   The clouds, the sun?

You must be lonely
   Amidst round trees
With their matron-figures
   And stubborn knees,
Casting hard glances
   Of keen despite
On the lone girl that dances
   Silvery white.

But you are dearer
   To sky and earth
Than lime-trees, plane-trees
   Of meaner birth.
Your sweet shy beauty
   Dearer to us
Than tree-folk, worthy,
   Censorious.

[10] GA: G.41.184.

November 1918 (KT)   19 Barton Street
                                                            Gloucester

My Dear Winnie

I hope you will like this book: it seems to me to be one of the jolliest and best packed books going.

Charles Doughty, Barrie, Housman (A E), Dr John Brown, G K C, Lucas, Sorley, Ledwidge, R. Bridges – let me especially recommend. I do hope all you lovely people will have a good time at High Wycombe since there are none better to deserve it; and O that I were along to share it with you, you dear children and grown ups! Alas there'll be no I.B.G. to smoke his churchwarden and deliver weighty sentences after the style of Dr Johnson. Someday, and soon, (for I am to return to College) St Mike's will shelter me once again, and O will there be ping-pong? Will the state of Europe permit frivolities, think you? Let's hope there will be a great flurry of snow that night to encircle the feasting house with white wonder untouched till Micky goes out to dance on it. That night Miss Marjory [*sic*] shall play Beethoven's most difficult Sonata and Arthur wriggle his eeliest. The fond parents looking on indulgently the while, bless 'em, for in calibre precision of fire and general aptitude for service they are level with the best. My best respex to you all and may you like this presink.

Yours affectionately
Ivor Gurney

A year earlier, in a letter to to Marion Scott, [11] Gurney had listed his chosen dedicatees for a projected second edition of *Severn and Somme*. 'Praise' was for Micky Chapman, and 'Carol' for Winnie.

Praise

O friends of mine, if men mock at my name,
Say 'Children loved him.'
Since by that word you will have far removed him
From any bitter shame.

[11] GA: G.41.158.

Carol

Winter now has bared the trees,
   Killed with tiny swords the jolly
Leafage that mid-summer sees,
   But left the ivy and the holly.
Hold them high
   And make delight
For Christë's joy that's born to-night.

All green things but these have hid
   Their heads, or died in melancholy,
Winter's spite them all has rid
   Save only ivy and brave holly.
Give them place
   In all men's sight
For Christë's grace that's born tonight.

Baby eyes are pleased to see
   Bright red berries and children jolly,
So shout and dance and sing with glee,
   And honour ivy and prickly holly.
Honour courage
   And make delight
For Christë's sake that's born to-night.

Christus natus hodie!
   Drink deep of joy on Christmas Day,
Join hands and sing a roundelay,
   For this is Christ's and children's day.
Christus natus hodie!
   Hodie!

POSTCARD from Stroud (A view of Stroud from Rodborough).
Postmark dated 17 December 1918.
Addressed to: Miss W Chapman
Miss M Chapman
St Michael's, etc.

Sorry not to send two[12] but alas, there's only a hapenny left (That's a bawbee to Scots). How are Christmas preparations going on? O but I'd like to be there to help!

I.B.G.

How's the piano Mick?

January 1919 (KT)

My Dear Old Win

O don't be sick, seedy, out of sorts and so on, for soon it is the intention of the famous composer to visit the Hill of the Castle with St Mike's situated thereon (its outhouses and messuages pertaining) and to find you not in a condition to play Ping-Pong would be sad indeed. Well, here's to a Happy New Year to you and all the rest with no crock-up and nothing but robust and even noisy health.

---

[12] Gurney sent one copy of *Severn and Somme*.

It's snowing hard outside. Snowing like blazes (to use an unsuitable simile) and lovely to look at the dark-sky world is. Can you send any hints on how to pack shirts, music, socks, books, coats, shoes, of enormous bulk into a box half the size of the combined mass? If so please do, for that is the problem that confronts me. Or hints how to write joyous Masterpieces when in the dumps? Ah, but you poor dear, having to lie still, and take things what they call 'easy' have none too good a time. May it pass, soon, soon! Dear kid, I am so glad you like that book. It is an honour to get in with such a select crowd, ain't it? Book 2 of me is at the publishers but no reply has been received as yet. Well, here's hopes to see the whole Joyful Crowd of you soon.

With love from your humble obedt servant
I.B.G.

4

POSTSCRIPT

Following his release from the Army, Gurney returned to his parents' home in Gloucester. His father was terminally ill, his mother preoccupied, and he met with resentment from his brother, Ronald, who had also served in the Army and probably considered Ivor's long hospitalisation to have been contrived to avoid further active service. Ronald, an intelligent man whose ambition to train as a doctor was frustrated by lack of means, cannot have understood the very real distress that Ivor was suffering. A signaller whose task it had been to maintain wireless contact under bombardment, straining to listen through headphones to messages disrupted by static, and required to crawl through mud to repair radio cables snapped by shellfire, Ivor was now plagued by imagined voices and by an inability to control his hopelessly irregular eating habits. On 6th October, John Haines explained the situation in a letter to Marion Scott:

I saw Ivor for most of yesterday. Perhaps you had best not tell him I have written to you. He spent an hour at the office and I was horrified – at all events at first. Quite evidently his trouble was on him especially badly at first, I thought him in a pretty serious way. After a while I began to see that his ideas about the voices and so forth, though extravagant, were in themselves ordered and sensible – granting the fact that they existed, and I became more comfortable. It was a beastly day but I cut the office and took him for a walk (rain or no rain) over the Cotswolds; Crickley, Birdlip and so forth, for the whole of the afternoon; tired myself out and I hope him. He was much more normal and left me happy enough with plenty of books and less annoyance from the voices – I think. I think something must be done with him soon. Is it any use for him to think of music or work connected therewith – yet? He talks of the sea. His shrunken appearance is not satisfactory, nor his quietness and humility. He left at 7 and I was so exhausted and drained that I slept the clock round![1]

Finding little affinity with his family at home, Gurney seriously considered going away to sea. Within a few days of his arrival in Gloucester, he went to Lydney in an effort to find a ship. Having no luck there he walked overnight the twenty-three miles to Newport – but again found no vessel to take him. He borrowed money and, the next day, returned to Gloucester, arriving back at lunchtime. That same afternoon Edward Chapman, arriving from High Wycombe to see Gurney, was saddened to learn of his condition. During a long discussion with the family, Chapman offered to adopt Ivor; a proposal that was unacceptable to the proud Gurneys. However, he was at least able to dissuade Ivor from his notions of going to sea. Throughout the afternoon Ivor remained calm and normal for the first time since leaving Napsbury, and the day ended happily with Ivor and his father walking back to Gloucester railway station to see Edward Chapman off.

[1] Michael Hurd, *op cit*, p. 128.

Friends rallied round, and at Christmas Ethel Voynich invited him to spend a few days with like-minded souls in Cornwall.

There the party went rock climbing at Gurnard Head, and, suddenly missing him in the gathering dusk, were astonished to find that he had climbed to the top of a narrow 'chimney' in the rocks, from which he had to be guided down by the experts among them. It turned out that he had been writing in his music notebook a setting of Francis Ledwidge's poem 'Desire in Spring'![2]

Gurney's return to creativity coincided with a marked improvement in his mental condition. So much so that he was able to withstand the sadness of the death of Margaret Hunt on 3rd March at the age of 44. She had succumbed to the Spanish influenza pandemic that began in April 1918 and for a year swept the world, claiming 25,000,000 victims. Then came good news: the Armistice, notification from Sidgwick & Jackson that his second volume of poems, *War's Embers*, had been accepted for publication, and Will Harvey returned from his long captivity in Germany. He too had suffered from influenza, and was still weak and jaundiced. Yet within a few weeks Gurney and Harvey were able to give a recital in Stroud:

[2] Francis Ledwidge (1887–1917) served in the 5th Battalion of the Royal Inniskilling Fusiliers and was killed on 31 July 1917 at the Carrefour des Roses in Boezinge.

S T A R S I N A D A R K N I G H T

From *The Stroud Journal*, 16th March 1919:

By the kindness of Miss Gorton, a number of Stroud residents were privileged to meet at the Sesame Shop on Saturday afternoon for one of the literary treats which her enterprise has provided from time to time. The poet Drinkwater has twice visited Stroud to read his poems, and on Saturday Lieut. F.W. Harvey, D.C.M., whose poetic muse was for a time confined in a German prison camp, recited his verses to a charmed audience. Lieut. Harvey was accompanied by Mr. Ivor Gurney, a musician of ability, who also developed the poet's art while serving in the army[. . .]

Mr Harvey said that in the first place poetry was chanted to the lyre, and he introduced to the audience Mr. Ivor Gurney, who had set to music some of his lyrics and would accompany him that afternoon. The recital was divided into the poet's Songs of Gloucestershire, Songs of the War, and Drinking Songs. Mr. Harvey first of all presented 'A Portrait' and followed with 'Piper's Wood' remarking that he was sure there was no county in England with such delightful place-names as Gloucestershire [. . .] Among the poems so skilfully set to music by Mr. Gurney and pleasantly sung by Mr. Harvey, were 'Horses', 'The Rest Farm', and 'Minsterworth Perry'. The poems of a convivial nature were presented with gusto, and Mr. Harvey's sense of humour was betrayed in many of his selections. Mr. Harvey and Mr. Gurney were sincerely thanked for their united efforts, and Miss Gorton for making possible such a delightful afternoon.

Haines attended the recital and reported that Gurney was 'wonderfully normal and well'.

As the months passed, with the help of friends such as Haines and Howells, Gurney's condition steadily improved. In the spring of 1919 he went to stay at Harvey's home, The Redlands, to share with Will the old inspiriting, healing pleasures of countryside and river. Gurney walked many miles, either alone or in the company of friends, and found that in the countryside and through physical exertion he could silence the 'voices' that tormented him. Unsurprisingly, he sought out hard manual labour, and in April worked for a few weeks at Dryhill Farm, near Witcombe in Gloucestershire.

On 10th May, David Gurney died at the age of fifty-seven, severing Ivor's strongest bond with his home. The Royal College of Music invited him to take up his scholarship once more, and later in the month he returned to London, this time to study with Dr Ralph Vaughan Williams. He rented rooms, first in Clifton Hill, St John's Wood, then in Winchester Road, Hampstead, and finally, the cheapest, in Earls Court. Eventually, he abandoned London lodgings altogether and moved out to 51 Queen's Road, High Wycombe, resuming his organ post at Christ Church and his close friendship with the Chapmans. Now followed one of the happiest, most fruitful and creative periods in Gurney's life.

The Chapmans welcomed Gurney back as a son to their midst. The joy in family life, the countryside, home-cooking, music-making, boisterous fun and gentle pleasure provided the perfect atmosphere in which he could both relax and find inspiration.

Following the publication of *War's Embers*, Gurney proudly presented a copy to: 'La Comtesse and the Chapman Family generally, with all good wishes for all sorts of good things – from the Admiring Author. May 1919'. Of these poems Gurney dedicated 'The Battalion is Now at Rest' to 'La Comtesse' and 'The Poplar' to Micky; he also dedicated piano pieces to Mrs Chapman – the Prelude in D flat – and to Winnie – the Prelude in D. His gifts to the Chapmans were usually books. For her birthday in August 1919 Winnie received one of Ivor's trench companions – a copy of *The Path to Rome* by Hilaire Belloc. At Christmas that year, Winnie was presented with the play *Abraham Lincoln* by John Drinkwater; Kitty with Masefield's *Saltwater Ballads*.

Gurney's music was now being performed, and gradually he began to enjoy the recognition of poets whom he admired, including Shanks, Gibson and Bridges. In April 1919 he returned the copy of *Deborah* that Catherine Abercrombie had sent to him, 'covered in authentic stains from the battlefields'.[3] Lascelles Abercrombie's letter of acknowledgement was in Winnie Chapman's possession, presumably left at High Wycombe by Gurney:

[3] See Jeff Cooper, 'Ivor Gurney and the Abercrombies', *The Ivor Gurney Society Journal*, vol. 9, 2003, p. 12.

Cloverfield , Dymock, Glos   Ap. 14

Dear Mr Gurney,

Many thanks for the *Deborah*: it will be a particularly precious memento, which my wife & I will be proud to treasure. You shall have a nice clean copy in exchange.

I am down here in this paradise alone – working: the rest of the family is in Grange, and I am going up there this week for Easter. I hope when I return it will not be long before we meet. My wife is coming down here for a week or so in May: I know she will hope to see you.

I am delighted you like that poem of mine – more than delighted with your comparisons: I wish I could do something I myself would dare to compare with Schubert's posthumous quartette or Mozart's G minor!

Yours sincerely,
Lascelles Abercrombie

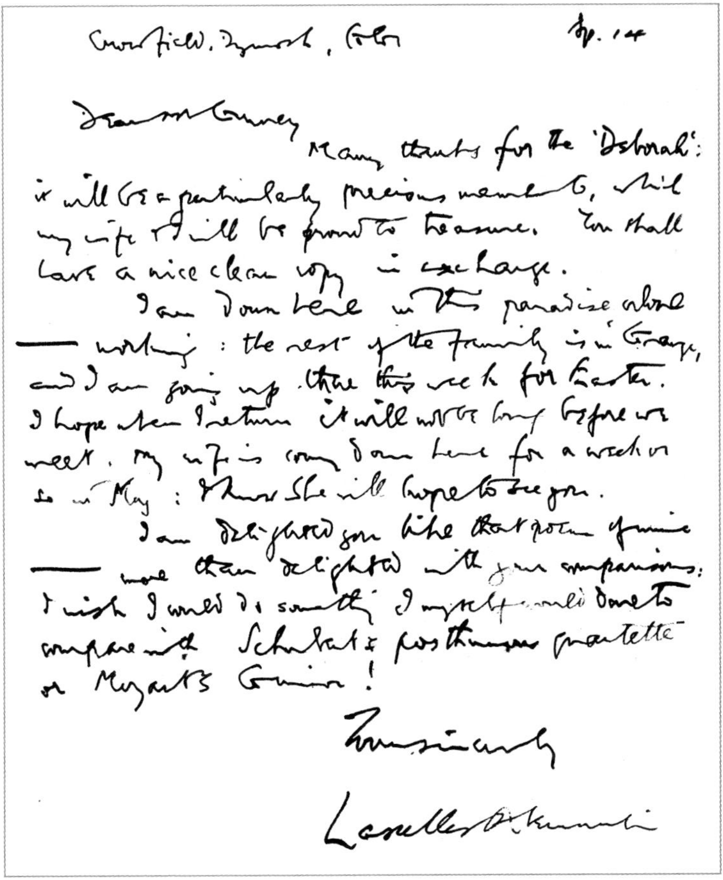

Crowfield, Dymock, Glos   Ap. 14

Dear Mr Gurney

Many thanks for the 'Deborah': it will be a particularly precious memento, which my wife & I will be proud to treasure. You shall have a nice clean copy in exchange.

I am down here in this paradise alone — working: the rest of the family is in Grange, and I am going up there this week for Easter. I hope when I return it will not be long before we meet. My wife is coming down here for a week or so in May: I know she will hope to see you.

I am delighted you like that poem of mine — more than delighted with your companions: I wish I could do something I myself could dare to compare with Schubert's posthumous quartette or Mozart's G minor!

Yours sincerely

Lascelles Abercrombie

In November 1919 Gurney and Harvey were invited by John Masefield to spend a day with him at his home at Boar's Hill, Oxford. Masefield thought *War's Embers* very good; he also enjoyed Gurney's settings of 'Captain Stratton's Fancy', 'The Halt of the Legion' and 'Upon the Downs', sung by Harvey, but was less impressed with 'By a Bierside'. This is odd, given that it is one of Gurney's very best songs – but an accomplished singer is needed if it is to make any impact, and perhaps Will Harvey was not that singer. Even so, given mental stability, it seems likely that Gurney could now have begun to take his rightful place as a dually gifted poet and composer of superb quality. Sadly, this was not to be.

As 1920 passed, Gurney spent less and less time at the RCM; a fellow student remembered how he was often self-absorbed. Ivor, a fine sportsman, was a member of the RCM football XI. On one occasion, when the team was to play an away game, a coach was laid on to take them to the ground outside London. When the time came for the coach to leave, Gurney failed to turn up, and after delaying their departure for some time, the other players were obliged to leave without him. It was a day of miserably wet weather, and when the coach arrived at its destination, there was Gurney, wedged into the hedge surrounding the field, sheltering from the rain under an oilskin cape and reading a book. He had cycled to the ground on his own, saying nothing to any of the others.[4]

To escape from London, he resumed his long hikes into the countryside, even walking as far as Gloucester.

---

[4] Reminiscences of Sir Keith Falkner (1900–1994).

Oct 24.

Roebuck Yard
7 in Market
Street, off
the Cornmarket
street.

BOAR'S HILL,
OXFORD.

Dear Mr Harvey,

Many thanks for your letter.

Will you come to lunch with us at 1 pm, on Sat, Nov 8th?

I hope that that will suit you comfortably.

There is a famous brake which leaves the Roebuck Hotel Yard at 12.30 daily. This will leave you close to my house in time for lunch. The Driver will tell you how to proceed when he puts you down.

We look forward to meeting you both. With best greetings,

Yours very truly John Masefield.

Invitation from John Masefield to F.W. Harvey and Ivor Gurney

Ivor Gurney with 'La Comtesse' and Micky in 1919

He needed the discipline of the RCM if he was ever to be able to achieve his potential in music – but his need for the inspiration that only Gloucestershire could provide was equally compelling. His wandering and 'nightwalking' resumed. At The Redlands, the Harvey family would prop open the dining room window for him before retiring to bed. Then, in the dead of night, Ivor would climb in, muddy from his travels, help himself from the pantry and play the piano for hours before snoozing in a chair. Unfortunately, Mrs Harvey's sister Kate Waters's bedroom was directly above the piano and she was less than appreciative of Ivor's renditions of Mozart sonatas, complaining bitterly to Will about the music disturbing her sleep. At last Will was obliged to tell Ivor that Auntie Kate objected to his

Ivor Gurney with 'La Comtesse' and Winnie in 1919

over-loud nocturnes. 'Oh, the world is *full* of Auntie Kates!' said Gurney.[5]

The Chapmans became increasingly concerned about Ivor's unpredictable behaviour. On one occasion, he arrived at St Michael's very late after everyone had gone to bed and, as at The Redlands but without permission, entered the house through the kitchen window, raided the pantry and ate a tin of biscuits before falling asleep, under Edward Chapman's overcoat, on a couch in the drawing room. When Chapman came down in the morning to find Gurney lying on the couch, surrounded by the remains of his

[5] Anthony Boden, *F.W. Harvey: Soldier, Poet* (Sutton, 1988, 2/1998), p. 258.

irregular supper, he angrily offered Gurney the rest of the family's coats and the keys to the cashbox. Distressed by what he had done, Gurney exclaimed: 'Oh dear, what an allotment'. But the anger was short-lived, and certainly not shared by the Chapman children, who thought the episode quite funny.

In April 1920 Gurney attended an ambitious Bach Festival, mounted over four days at the Central Hall, Westminster, under the direction of Hugh Allen. The Bach Choir, the London Symphony Orchestra, and a galaxy of eminent soloists appeared in a series of concerts devoted to the music of the Master, culminating on the evening of Tuesday 20th April with what must have been a magnificent performance of the *Mass in B minor*. Following the event, Gurney presented the lavishly produced programme book of the Festival to Micky Chapman, adding the inscription:

'To MC from IBG – May 1920 – with exhortation'.

Gurney had recognised Micky's potential as a pianist, and the exhortation was, of course, that she should work hard at her music. In October 1919 he had sketched a short *Album Leaf* for her fingers, and when his song 'Desire in Spring' was published in December 1920 in *The Chapbook*, the journal of the Poetry Bookshop in Devonshire Street, Ivor gave a copy 'To Micky Chapman, with the best of wishes, Christmas 1920'. His 'exhortation' was certainly to bear fruit: Micky eventually followed Ivor to the Royal College, gaining her ARCM in 1931.

The years 1919 and 1920 were years of intense creativity for Gurney. Composing at white heat, he completed sixty songs in 1920 alone, saying to his friends 'Words, I must have words'! In addition, he

Ivor Gurney at St Michael's, 1919

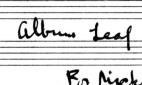

completed a string quartet, pieces for piano, the orchestral *War Elegy*, and was working on the major song cycles *Ludlow and Teme* and *The Western Playland*, the first of which is an undoubted masterpiece.

But, try as he might, Gurney was unable to hold down any sort of permanent employment. He took odd labouring jobs on farms, worked briefly in a cold storage depot in London, played the piano in cinemas at Plumstead and Bude, but all to no avail – every attempt ended in speedy dismissal.

In the summer of 1921, Ivor finally left the RCM and returned to Gloucester to live with his aunt, Edith Gurney, at 1 Westfield Terrace, Longford, on the northern outskirts of the city. Soon, the dreadful voices in his head returned, along with the added torment of imagined bombardment by wireless waves. In spite of this, he continued to work at composition, including a set of *Five Pastorals* ('Children's Pieces') that he copied out neatly and gave to Micky.

Gurney's condition continued to deteriorate markedly; his 'nightwalking' and dishevelled appearance prompting harsh comments from the Westfield Terrace neighbours who, espying his comings and goings from behind net curtains, feared that there was a madman at No.1. How could they know that Gurney was only able to maintain any kind of grip on his mental stability, and thus his creativity, *because* of his wanderings and closeness to nature?

Desperate for suitable paid employment, Gurney wrote to Edward Marsh in June 1922:

[. . .] If you could help me to a clerkship at the Income Tax Office in Gloucester I should feel very obliged. Both the age and the ERA reject me, and in any case a picture palace was not the best of jobs. A clerkship would leave me without ties, with enough time to get and to keep health. At present the county seems too lovely to leave. I seem to have caused a lot of people a lot of trouble, but think that the whole lump of my songs is the best of any lump. Reading accounts of new masterpieces brought out in London is disturbing, but there . . . The County and English Literature should keep one sane. Mr Kerr, head of the Department knows me personally, and backs my application. From the tales of ignorance shown by the girl clerks I should be worth the money I think, and until a lectureship or a good school job (neither likely) comes along I should consider myself lucky to have it.[6]

---

[6] New York Public Library Berg Collection.

Ivor Gurney at 1, Westfield Terrace, Longford, Gloucester, 1921

Marsh contacted William (Pat) Kerr, an acquaintance of Gurney's since before the war and a minor poet whose work was to be published, at Gurney's recommendation, in the fifth volume of *Georgian Poetry*. Kerr was a civil servant, a literary talker and a writer of style and wit who was to become leader-writer for the *Yorkshire Post* and literary critic of the *Gloucester Journal*. Ivor was given a job as a tax clerk in Gloucester, but alas, even that lasted only three months. Whilst at work he had complained of interference by wireless messages. His erratic eating habits descended to near-starvation, and by August, having eaten practically nothing for two weeks, Ronald

Ronald Gurney

Gurney was summoned to the Tax Office to escort his brother back to Longford.

The family GP, Dr Cairns Terry, was called. He recommended that Gurney should be admitted to Barnwood House, a mental hospital near Gloucester (now demolished). Instead, he was sent to a convalescent home for 'neurasthenics' near Bristol, but within a fortnight the authorities there recognised that Gurney's case was beyond their competence. He was returned to Gloucester and moved in with Ronald and his new bride, Ethel Gurney, who lived at 52 Worcester Street.

Since the death of his father, Ronald had reluctantly taken over the family business, moving the tailoring workshop to the ground floor of the Worcester Street house, and cycling over to the city shop each day with completed garments. If the sudden arrival of Ivor was in itself unwelcome, his continued presence soon proved to be intolerable. Wandering abroad until the small hours; coming in long after Ronald and Ethel had retired to bed; entering their bedroom and scrabbling about in search of a candle; curling up in an armchair, a cushion pressed over his ears in an attempt to keep out the imagined radio waves; and leaving mud from his shoes on the best furniture, were all manifestations of a disturbed mind beyond the understanding of the tailor of Gloucester and his wife.

Within weeks, Ivor's behaviour could no longer be tolerated by his family. He was certified insane and committed to Barnwood House on 28th September with a diagnosis of 'systematised delusional insanity'. Whilst there he made two unsuccessful attempts at escape: once by climbing over the railings, and a second, on 8th November, when he smashed a locked

Ivor Gurney on a visit to Knole, Kent, late 1920s.
(Photograph Marion Scott)

window by throwing a large clock through it and, climbing out, cut himself badly on the broken glass.

Meanwhile, in London, Marion Scott was organising a fund to assist in Gurney's financial support. Vaughan Williams, Arthur Benjamin, Walter de la Mare and Marion Scott herself all made donations, and a grant was made by Sir Alexander Butterworth, the father of the composer George Butterworth, who had lost his life at Pozières in 1916. Miss Scott also took the initiative in arranging for Gurney to be transferred from Barnwood House to a hospital nearer to the capital, where she and his London friends could visit him, and from where, she believed, he would be able to take his proper place in the artistic life of the city once he had recovered from his illness – and where he would be far removed from family pressures.

On 21st September 1922, Gurney was taken to the City of London Mental Hospital at Dartford, Kent. Release never came – he was to remain there for fifteen years until his death on 26th December 1937.

Throughout those long years, Marion Scott was Gurney's most frequent visitor. Others came too, especially in the early years – Ralph Vaughan Williams, Herbert Howells, Arthur Benjamin, Edward Chapman and Gurney's mother all travelled down to Dartford – but as the twenties gave way to the thirties, fewer and fewer made the journey, until only Howells and Marion Scott were prepared to face the ordeal.

Marion Scott was occasionally able to arrange outings in a chauffeur-driven car for Ivor and herself, permitted only if Gurney was accompanied by a male nurse. They went to the Old Vic Theatre on one occasion, to Knole

Park, and to the Kent home of Mrs Hester Stansfield Prior, who recorded her impressions of the visit:

Though I knew and admired many of the poems and songs written by Ivor Gurney before the 1914–18 war, I did not meet him till much later when, owing to the cruel injuries of war – both mental and physical – his career as a musician ended. He had already been under constant medical supervision for several years at the time of his first visit to me with Miss Marion Scott. With the idea of at once arousing interest, scores, Pianoforte music and songs were artfully placed where they might catch his eye, and before long he sat down at the piano. After playing a few chords, he asked to hear a Beethoven sonata; Op.110 was my reply. Next, some vocal scores were required, from which (so far as I remember) he played favourite passages from Elgar and talked about *leitmotifs*.

Ivor's second visit took place nearly two years later. As neither myself nor the house were any longer strange to him, we started at once with a Haydn symphony, arranged for Pianoforte duet. Seeing that he was completely out of practice, his reading was excellent but he tired before the last movement and said that he 'preferred Brahms'. Encouraged and helped by Miss Scott, he eventually chose the E minor Symphony from a pile of Brahms's music and, from the miniature score, proceeded to make a remarkable transcription of the work. The tempi were all beyond criticism, no theme was overlooked, and details were filled in to an extent that might have been envied by many a musician in full practice. One of the most moving recollections of my life is that of Ivor wrestling with the slow movement, (the only one he played throughout) and of his obvious annoyance that all details could not be included on the piano.

Another side to his life was shown in a summertime visit to my garden, where a small bowls green attracted his attention. In his time he had been a keen footballer, so was quite ready to learn a new game. His look of pleasure when he made a successful shot, and his appreciative 'good' when his opponent did the same, are unforgettable.[7]

On the way back to Dartford in the car, Marion Scott, pointing to the sky, said 'Oh look, Ivor, isn't that a lovely sunset?' 'I don't know', replied the poet of the stars and skies, 'I don't see them any more'.

In an essay in the Easter 1960 issue of the RCM magazine, Helen, the widow of Edward Thomas, recalled her harrowing visits to Gurney at Dartford:

[. . .] We arrived at the asylum which looked like – as indeed it was – a prison. A warder let us in after unlocking a door, and doors were opened and locked behind us as we were ushered into the building. We were walking along a bare corridor when we were met by a tall gaunt dishevelled man clad in pyjamas and dressing gown, to whom Miss Scott introduced me. He gazed with an intensive stare into my face and took me silently by the hand. Then I gave him the flowers which he took with the same deeply moving intensity and silence. He then said: 'You are

[7] GA: G.75.3.

Helen, Edward's wife and Edward is dead.' I said, 'Yes, let us talk of him.' So we went into a little cell-like bedroom where the only furniture was a bed and a chair. The window was barred and the walls were bare and drab. He put the flowers on the bed for there was no vessel to put them in; there was nothing in the room that could in any way be used to do damage with – no pottery or jars whose broken edge could be used as a weapon. He remarked on my pretty hat, for it was summer and I had purposely put on my prettiest clothes. The gay colours gave him pleasure. I sat by him on the bed and we talked of Edward and myself, but I cannot now remember the conversation. But I do remember that though his talk was quite sane and lucid, he said 'It was wireless that killed Edward', and this idea of the danger of wireless and his fear of it constantly occurred in his talk. 'They are getting at me through wireless.' We spoke of country that he knew and which Edward knew too and he evidently identified Edward with the English countryside, especially that of Gloucestershire. I learned from the warder that Ivor Gurney refused to go into the grounds of the asylum. It was not his idea of countryside – the fields and woods and footpaths he loved so well – and he would have nothing to do with this travesty of something that was sacred to him. Before we left he took us into a large room in which was a piano and on this he played to us and the tragic circle of men who sat on hard benches against the walls of the room. Hopeless and aimless faces gazed vacantly and restless hands fumbled or hung down lifelessly. They gave no sign or sound that they heard the music. The room was quite bare and there wasn't one beautiful thing for the patients to look at.

We left and I promised to come again.

Ivor Gurney longed more than anything else to go back to his beloved Gloucestershire, but this was not allowed for fear he should try to take his own life. I said 'But surely it would be more humane to let him go there even if it meant no more than one hour of happiness before he killed himself.' But the authorities could not look at it in that way.

The next time I went with Miss Scott I took with me one of Edward's own well-used ordnance maps of Gloucester where he had often walked. This proved to have been a sort of inspiration, for Ivor at once spread them out on his bed and he and I spent the whole time I was there tracing with our fingers the lanes and byeways and villages of which he knew every step and over which Edward had walked. He spent that hour in re-visiting his beloved home, in spotting a village or a track, a hill or a wood and seeing it all in his mind's eye, a mental vision sharper and more actual for his heightened intensity. He trod, in a way we who are sane could not emulate, the lanes and fields he knew and loved so well, his guide being his finger tracing the way on the map. It was deeply moving, and I knew that I had hit on an idea that gave him more pleasure than anything else I could have thought of. For he had Edward as his companion in this strange perambulation and he was utterly happy.

This way of using my visits was repeated several times and I became for a while not a visitor from the outside world of war and wireless, but the element which brought Edward back to life for him and the country where the two could wander together.

Whenever Will Harvey visited Dartford he found a tortured soul pleading for liberty or death. 'Get me out of here, Willy!' his friend would say,[8] but Harvey knew that release would never come:

[8] Eileen Griffiths reminiscences.
[9] F.W. Harvey, 'To Ivor Gurney'.

Now hawthorn hedges live again;
　　And all along the banks below
Pale primrose fires have lit the lane
　　Where oft we wandered long ago
　　And saw the blossom blow.

And talked and walked till stars pricked out,
　　And sang brave midnight snatches under
The moon, with never a dread nor doubt,
　　Nor warning of that devil's wonder
　　That tore our lives asunder.

And left behind a nightmare trail
　　Of horrors scattered through the brain,
Of shattered hopes and memories frail
　　That bloom like flowers in some old lane
　　And tear the heart in twain.

This hawthorn hedge will bank its snow
　　Spring after Spring, and never care
What song and dreams of long ago
　　Within its shade were fashioned fair
　　Of happy air.

But you within the madhouse wall,
　　But you and I who went so free,
Never shall keep Spring's festival
　　Again, though burgeon every tree
　　With blossom joyously.

Not that I fear to keep the faith;
　　Not that my heart goes cravenly;
But that some voice within me saith
　　'The Spring is dead!' yea, dead, since he
　　Will come no more to me.

It needeth but a tear to quench
　　The primrose fires: to melt the snow
Of Spring-time hedges, and to drench
　　With black the blue clear heavens show . . .
　　And I have wept for you.[9]

Gurney composed no more music after 1926 but continued to write poetry – a steady stream, both of complete poems and verse-pieces. When he died, on 26 December 1937, he was forty-seven years old and had spent fifteen of those years within asylum walls.

Now, at last, he was permitted to return home – to be buried in the little graveyard at St Matthew's Church, Twigworth, just outside Gloucester, where his godfather, Alfred Cheesman, was rector. Cheesman conducted the service, Herbert Howells played the organ, and Will Harvey was among the small congregation of mourners. Standing at the sad winter graveside, Harvey took from his pocket a tiny sprig of rosemary, plucked at Minsterworth that morning, and dropped it down on to the lid of the lowered coffin; tied to it was a small label upon which he had written: 'Rosemary for Remembrance'.

*   *   *   *

In the introduction to his collection of poems by Ivor Gurney,[10] Leonard Clark concluded that: 'The pity is for Ivor Gurney himself whose generation did not know that he was burning and palpitating in their midst, with a fiery brain and heart, singing songs of the heart's pain and the world's loveliness, and hating what man's wars had done to man'. Indeed, if it had not been for the efforts of Marion Scott it is doubtful that any of Gurney's work would have survived. He sent her all of his manuscripts: the poems, which she arranged to have typed, and the music, which she carefully

[10] Leonard Clark, *Poems of Ivor Gurney* (Chatto & Windus, 1973).

stored in a secure chest. She it was who arranged the publication of *Severn and Somme* and *War's Embers*; she too who first secured publication of any of his songs; and she it was who visited and supported him financially throughout the asylum years. However, she made no attempt to catalogue the mass of Gurney's work in her possession.

In spite of the approval received from established poets, such as Robert Bridges and Walter de la Mare, few of Gurney's poems appeared in print after 1919. It seems that his generation was indeed prepared to allow his work and the memory of him to fade into obscurity – but one man was intent on rescue.

In 1920, the young composer Gerald Finzi (1901–1956), whilst in York, heard Gurney's song 'Sleep' for the first time, sung by Elsie Suddaby in one of Edward Bairstow's voice lessons.[11] He felt immediately that it was one of *the* great songs, written with such intensity of feeling that it was 'not being wise after the event to say that one can feel an incandescence in his songs that tells of something burning too brightly to last, such as you see in the filament of an electric light bulb before it burns out'.[12] This revelation led him to investigate Gurney's work, and for the rest of his short life, with the assistance of his friend Howard Ferguson, he worked to bring Marion Scott's collection to public attention. Two volumes, each of ten Gurney songs, were published by OUP in 1938; a third followed in

[11] Finzi was a private pupil of Bairstow, the organist of York Minster.

[12] Gerald Finzi, 'The composer's use of words': [three] Crees Lectures, *RCM* (typescript, 1955). See also Stephen Banfield, *Gerald Finzi; An English Composer* (Faber & Faber, 1997), p. 393.

Gerald Finzi

1952, the year before the death of Marion Scott; and in 1954, two years before his own premature death, Finzi initiated the publication of seventy-eight poems, selected and introduced by Edmund Blunden;[13] the book is dedicated to:

> THE MEMORY OF MARION M. SCOTT
> (1877–1953)
> A GENEROUS AND CONSTANT FRIEND
> WHOSE REGARD FOR THE WELFARE
> OF IVOR GURNEY AND
> PRESERVATION OF HIS MANUSCRIPTS
> ENABLED THIS FIRST SELECTION
> TO BE MADE

And what of the Chapmans? In 1923 the Great Western Railway transferred Edward Chapman to the post of Goods Manager at Gloucester – Ivor's Gloucester. The family moved into Cranham House, Churchdown, at the foot of Chosen Hill where Gurney had walked with Howells, gazing out over the Severn Vale to the distant Malverns.

By sheer coincidence, Gerald Finzi and his mother had taken a holiday at Churchdown in the summer of 1920; they returned in March 1921, this time to lodge at Chosen Hill House. (Chosen Hill was the source of inspiration for Finzi's cantata *In Terra Pax*, when, after a party on Christmas Eve in the tiny sexton's cottage beside the little church on the hill, they 'had all come out into the frosty midnight and heard bells ringing

---

[13] Edmund Blunden (ed.), *Poems of Ivor Gurney* (Hutchinson, 1954).

Chosen Hill, Chuchdown, Gloucestershire

The Chapmans with a friend, Miss Colwell, at Cranham House,
Churchdown

Winnie and Micky

across Gloucestershire from beside the Severn to the hill villages of the Cotswolds'.[14])

The Chapmans missed seeing Ivor, who had already been taken to Dartford by the time they arrived in Gloucestershire. After the spring of 1921 his visits to St Michael's had become less frequent. By then, Kitty was married, Winnie and Arthur had grown up, and Micky was 14.

One day, after he had not been to see the Chapmans for some weeks, Winnie saw Ivor walking towards her as she rode her bicycle into High Wycombe. His face was full of despair. Winnie stopped her bicycle and said: 'Oh, Ivor, whatever is the matter?' Tears welled up in his eyes. Looking away, he made a little gesture of hopelessness with his hand and walked quickly on without a word. Winnie never saw him again.

[14] Stephen Banfield, *op cit*, p. 96.

To God

Why have you made life so intolerable
And set me between four walls, where I am able
Not to escape meals without prayer, for that is possible
Only by annoying an attendant. And tonight a sensual
Hell has been put upon me, so that all has deserted me
And I am merely crying and trembling in heart
For death, and cannot get it. And gone out is part
Of sanity. And there is dreadful hell within me.
And nothing helps. Forced meals there have been and electricity
And weakening of sanity by influence
That's dreadful to endure. And there is Orders
And I am praying for death, death, death,
And dreadful is the indrawing or outbreathing of breath
Because of the intolerable insults put on my whole soul,
Of the soul loathed, loathed, loathed of the soul.
Gone out every bright thing from my mind.
All lost that ever God himself designed.
Not half can be written of cruelty of man, on man,
Not often such evil guessed as between man and man.

5

'THE SPRINGS OF MUSIC'

An Essay by Ivor Gurney

Ivor Gurney's essay 'The Springs of Music' was published in the United States of America in The Musical Quarterly *of July 1922. It is reproduced in full here for the first time in the United Kingdom.*

THE SPRINGS OF MUSIC

By Ivor Gurney

Since the springs of music are identical with those of the springs of all beauty remembered by the heart, an essay with this title can be little more than a personal record of visions of natural fairness remembered, it may be, long after bodily seeing.

It is the fact that these visions were more clearly seen after the excessive bodily fatigue experienced on a route march, or in some hard fatigue in France or Flanders – a compensation for so much strain. One found them serviceable in the accomplishment of the task, and in after-relaxation. There it was one learnt that the brighter visions brought music; the fainter verse, or mere pleasurable emotion.

Of all significant things the most striking, poignant, passioning, is the sight of a great valley at the end of the day – such as the Severn Valley which lies hushed and dark, infinitely full of meaning, while the yet far Welsh hills are touched with living and ecstatic gold. The first breakings of the air of night, the remembrance of the glory not all yet faded; the meeting of the two pageants of day and night so powerfully stir the heart that music alone may assuage its thirst, or satisfy that longing told by Wordsworth in the *Prelude*; but that telling and outpouring of his is but the shadow and faint far-off indication of what Music might do – the chief use of Poetry seeming to be, to one, perhaps

THE MUSICAL QUARTERLY

O. G. SONNECK, *Editor*

VOL. 8, No. 3   JULY, 1922

CONTENTS

PUBLISHED QUARTERLY

THREE DOLLARS A YEAR   At 3 East 43d Street   SEVENTY-FIVE CENTS A COPY
New York, N. Y.

Entered as second-class matter December 31, 1914, at the Post Office at New York, N. Y.,
under the Act of March 3, 1879.

G. SCHIRMER, Inc. NEW YORK

mistaken, musician, to stir his spirit to the height of music, the maker to create, the listener worthily to receive or remember.

The quietest and most comforting thing that is yet strongly suggestive – the sight which seems more than any to provoke the making of music to be performed on strings, is that of a hedge mounting over, rolling beyond the skyline of a little gracious hill. A hedge unclipped, untamed; covered with hawthorn perhaps, showing the fragile rose of June, or sombre with the bareness of Winter; the season makes no difference. So that the hedge be of some age and the hill friendly enough of aspect, smooth, strokable, as it were, there is no end to the quiet suggestion, the subdued yet still quick power of the sight.

What may not be taken from a road winding over against a West clear beneath, above crowned with dark angerful clouds? To walk there, having seen sunset pass – 'the brands of sunset fall, flicker and fade from out the West,' as a poet has said – to top the hill and take on his face the last of the sunset wind, the first of the night. And to pass on, see groups of quiet voiced cottagers talking at gates not iron but of friendly wood, surrounded by peace and a fragrance of honeysuckle or some such tender thing. This is to know where so much of Schumann's music had its source.

Beethoven comes with the majesty of a wide plain on a blowy day, ruled imperiously by hills but afar off – kingly-wise but in temperate fashion. A plain roofed by the blue and cloud dappled, gloriously changing, swept clean by wind loving yet rough, austere yet friendly. Or his is the sight of a heaven of stars, seen from high above the world; alone at midnight one must stand

Ivor Gurney, *c.* 1921
(Photograph: Richard Hall)

where long ago the Romans kept their watch, and knew either bare slopes or beech boughs sawing backwards and forwards against the dim blue and the starry points thereon. It is right that one should wish to understand at least one of Beethoven's moods; should wrap himself in one of the Master's moods on such a place as Painswick Beacon, when nothing human is abroad, not a light in the valley save in the distant town; when no sound comes to the bodily ear save that ghostly one of the owl.

A copse is full of infinite suggestion of Schubert, and if it were threaded by some tiny dancing stream running sunlit water like some strange and splendid metal . . . Birds talk and sing there, and the Unfinished Symphony confirms one in wonder at the day's hotter hours.

Brahms has more of Autumn in him – the full coloured new ploughed earth also; rich-tinted, strongly fragrant soil unplanted. He has given us even the smell of leaves, it seems to myself at least; as in the Piano Quintet in F minor.[1]

Orchards are the inspiration of so much; blossom has borne blossom of song so many times in so many men. 'Adelaide', the First Rasoumoffsky Quartet,[2] Schubert's songs, Schumann's songs and the short pianoforte pieces, the songs of Brahms. . . . Who has not felt the spell of Spring so strongly symbolised herein?

As for the Sea, it has too little influenced or inspired the Makers of Song. Vaughan Williams alone has worthily expressed his mood of glory at the scent,

[1] Presumably, Gurney is referring to the Piano Quartet in A Major (the 'Trout' Op.114); A major is the relative key to F sharp minor.
[2] Both the song and the quartet are by Beethoven; the latter his Opus 59 in F major.

sound, sight of that infinite and unweakening wonder.[3] The Germans seem to care little for the sea, and anyhow the centres that drew their great musicians were far enough from blue water. The mountains must supply that need of complete grandeur which thrusts a snowy peak high out of the score, even the notes read merely, of Eroica or Coriolanus.[4]

In Bach is fairy tale, firelight, Cathedral space (of this a great deal), much human friendliness. The common intercourse of life, but raised high. An almost unparalleled grandeur is his at times, but seeming to come rather from ordered stone than the free majesty of mountain places, the sky or the sea. Yet such a man made out of Talking sunlit water the Italian Concerto, and – as for the Chromatic Fantasia, of what was such a huge wonder born? Of sheer cliffs or a thought of the battle of good and evil in some mighty heart? None can say; it is with far more than the common gratitude that we accept such things. The Ninth Symphony[5] begins with the mightiest of battle gatherings, and has the most tremendous of onslaughts in the few pages of its first movement. There the sky rages also as in King Lear; there the spirit of man realises its impotency yet eternal power of defiance before the forces of nature. Challenges, accepts and both powerfully, with dignity, and though certain in the end of doom, looks up at the ordered troops of dark cloud, and says, 'We are, but I shall be'.

From poplars has come much: the larch has given

---

[3] Vaughan Williams, *A Sea Symphony*, words by Walt Whitman.
[4] Both by Beethoven: Symphony No. 3 ('Eroica') and the Coriolan Overture.
[5] Beethoven: Symphony No. 9 ('The Choral').

grace to thought in many of the smaller forms. The oak has strengthened many, and in the shady chambers of the elm many have found peace. Trees are the friendliness of things, and the beech with its smooth A major trunk, its laughing E major foliage; the Scotch fir which passionate or still is always F sharp minor, cannot have been without influence on men.

Autumn is strongest in memory of all seasons. To think of Autumn is to be smitten through most powerfully with an F sharp minor chord that stops the breath, wrings the heart with unmeasurable power. On Brahms it is strong, this royal season; has given him much, worthily and truly translated. What! Do you not know the Clarinet Quintet, the Handel Variations, the C minor Symphony? And do you not smell Autumn air keen in the nostrils, touch and wonder at leaves fallen or about to fall? Have you not hastened to the woods of the F minor Quintet?[6]

Perhaps you are too enamoured of the April of Mozart, in which you are both right and wrong. His is 'the cascade of the larch'. The young heavens forgetful after rain. Arcady is his, and in the springing season.

Children are always a delight, but the large eyes and innocence of them are not Mozart's only, but of Schubert, Schumann, Haydn, and almost supremely of Bach, when he chooses to be fascinated by them. What is the little Prelude and Fugue in G major in the second part of the '48', but a fairy tale for children?[7]

[6] Brahms: Piano Quintet in F minor, Op. 34.
[7] J.S. Bach: *Das Wohltempierte Klavier II* (*The Well-tempered Clavier, Book II*), Prelude and Fugue XV in G major.

And who but a child brought the A major Concerto to us, or the F sharp Piano Sonata? (Of Mozart and Beethoven).

Firelight is infinitely strong on us all, but on Schumann pre-eminently. One would think that man to have known Cotswold, and to have sheltered from its winter air in a house built of the stone most worthily used for Cathedrals, and as perfectly built. To have watched the dance and interlacing of shadows on the dim walls, but most to have gazed and lost himself in the deepest heart of the log fire roaring upwards towards the vast chimney and the frosty stars.

This queer discursive essay-thing has come from remembrance of natural beauty which has brought music, and music that opened suddenly a pathway through to show some picture, long ago seen, it may be, but passioned, made mystic and far more dear from the unexpectedness of the gift. A beauty out of beauty suddenly thrust unasked upon a heart that dared not want more; had not dreamed of asking more, and was suddenly given completely eternal right in Cranham, Portway, Redmarley, Crickley – before, the Paradise of Earth; after, as things unearthly, not to be thought on without tears, nor a fear of loss known deep in the spirit to be unfounded, unbelievable.

Worse nonsense has been written about such things as we all believe, and though truth is better treated more honestly, yet even through this mist of pretty words may show some of the plainness of the truth as it may have seemed to the makers and receivers.

Poem for End

So the last poem is laid flat in its place,
And Crickley with Crucifix corner leaves from my face
Elizabethans and night-working thoughts – of such grace.

And all the dawns that set my thoughts new to making;
Or Crickley dusk that the beech leaves stirred to shaking
Are put aside – there is a book ended; heart aching.

Joy and sorrow, and all thoughts a poet thinks,
Walking or turning to music; the wrought-out links
Of fancy to fancy – by Severn or by Artois brinks.

Only what's false in this, blood itself would not save,
Sweat would not heighten – the dead Master in his grave
Would my true following of him, my care approve.

And more than he, I paid the prices of life
Standing where Rome immortal heard October's strife,
A war poet whose right of honour cuts falsehood like a knife.

War poet – his right is of nobler steel – the careful sword –
And night walker will not suffer of praise the word
From the sleepers, the custom-followers, the dead lives unstirred.

Only, who thought of England as two thousand years
Must keep of today's life the proper anger and fears:
England that was paid for by building and ploughing and tears.

Selected Bibliography

Ivor Gurney, *Severn and Somme* (Sidgwick & Jackson, 1917).

Ivor Gurney, *War's Embers* (Sidgwick & Jackson, 1919).

Ivor Gurney, 'The Springs of Music', *The Musical Quarterly*, VIII, No.3, July 1922.

Edmund Blunden (ed.), *The Poems of Ivor Gurney* (Hutchinson, 1954).

Leonard Clark (ed.), *Poems of Ivor Gurney 1890–1937* (Chatto & Windus, 1973).

Michael Hurd, *The Ordeal of Ivor Gurney* (OUP, 1978; paperback 1984).

P.J. Kavanagh (ed.), *Collected Poems of Ivor Gurney* (OUP, 1982; rev. edn. Carcanet/Fyfield Books, 2004).

P.J. Kavanagh (ed.), *Ivor Gurney – Selected Poems* (OUP, 1990).

Charles W. Moore, *Ivor Gurney, poet and songwriter* (Triad Press, 1976).

R.K.R. Thornton (ed.), *Ivor Gurney – War Letters* (MidNAG/Carcanet, 1983).

R.K.R. Thornton (ed.), *Ivor Gurney – Collected Letters* (MidNAG/Carcanet, 1991).

R.K.R. Thornton (ed.), *Ivor Gurney: Severn and Somme/War's Embers* (MidNAG Carcanet, 1987; paperback 1997).

R.K.R. Thornton and George Walter (eds.), *Ivor Gurney – Best Poems* and *The Book of Five Makings* (MidNAG/Carcanet, 1995).

George Walter and R.K.R. Thornton (eds.), *Ivor Gurney – 80 Poems or So* (MidNAG/Carcanet, 1997).

George Walter (ed.), *Ivor Gurney* (Everyman's Poetry, 1996).

George Walter (ed.), *Ivor Gurney – Rewards of Wonder* (MidNAG/Carcanet, 2000).

R.K.R. Thornton and Lynn Parker (eds.), *The Ivor Gurney Society Journal.* (The Journal has been published annually since 1995).

R.K.R. Thornton and George Walter, *Ivor Gurney: Towards a Bibliography* (The Ivor Gurney Society, 1996).

Stephen Banfield, *Sensibility and English Song* (OUP, 1983).

Anthony Boden, *F.W. Harvey: Soldier, Poet* (Sutton, 1988; 2/1998).

Jeremy Dibble, C., *Hubert H. Parry: His Life and Music* (OUP, 1992).

Robert Giddings, *The War Poets* (Bloomsbury, 1988).

Trevor Hold, *Parry to Finzi: Twenty English Song Composers* (Boydell, 2002).

John Lucas, *Ivor Gurney* (Writers and their Work series, British Council/Northcote House, 2001).

Christopher Palmer, *Herbert Howells: A Centenary Celebration* (Thames, 1992).

Michael Pilkington, *English Solo Song Guides: Gurney, Ireland, Quilter, and Warlock* (Duckworth, 1989; republished Thames/Elkin).

Paul Spicer, *Herbert Howells* (Seren, Borderlines series, 1998).

Jon Stallworthy, *Anthem for Doomed Youth: Twelve Soldier Poets of the First World War* (Constable, 2002).